Wealthier

Also by Daniel R. Solin

Does Your Broker Owe You Money?
The Smartest Investment Book You'll Ever Read
The Smartest 401(k) Book You'll Ever Read
The Smartest Money Book You'll Ever Read
The Smartest Portfolio You'll Ever Own
The Smartest Money Book You'll Ever Read
Timeless Investment Advice
7 Steps to Save Your Financial Life Now
The Smartest Sales Book You'll Ever Read
Ask: How to Relate to Anyone

To contact the author

Dan Solin
dansolin@ebadvisormarketing.com
https://wealthierbook.com/

Wealthier

The
Investing
Field Guide
for
Millennials

Wealthier — Copyright © Daniel R. Solin, 2024

Silvercloud Publishing, LLC
Bonita Springs, FL 34135

Paperback ISBN: 978-0-9748763-3-7
eBook ISBN: 978-0-9748763-4-4
Audiobook ISBN: 978-0-9748763-5-1

Library of Congress Control Number: 2024902764

Solin, Daniel R.
Wealthier/Daniel R. Solin
Includes bibliographical references and index

Cover design and interior layout: Language Arts

Printed in the United States of America
Publisher's Cataloging-in-Publication data
First Edition

All Rights Reserved. This publication may not be reproduced, stored in a retrieval system, or transmitted in whole or in part, in any form or by any means, electronic, mechanical, photocopying, recording, or otherwise — with the exception of a reviewer who may quote brief passages in a review to be printed in a newspaper or magazine — without prior written permission from the publisher.

This publication contains the opinions and ideas of its author and is designed to provide useful advice in regard to the subject matter covered. The author and publisher are not engaged in rendering financial, investing, social, counseling, psychological, psychiatric, medical, diagnostic, or other professional services in this publication. This publication is not intended to provide a basis for action in particular circumstances without consideration by a competent professional. The author and publisher expressly disclaim any responsibility for any liability, loss or risk, personal or otherwise, which may be incurred as a consequence, directly or indirectly, of the use and application of any of the contents of this book.

For permission requests, quantity sales, branding opportunities, strategic alliances, partnerships, media inquiries, speaking engagements, and orders by U.S. trade bookstores and wholesalers, please contact:

Dan Solin
dansolin@ebadivsormarketing.com
(239) 949-1606

Wealthier

The
Investing
Field Guide
for
Millennials

Daniel R. Solin
New York Times Bestselling Author of the *Smartest* Series of Books

Disclaimer

This book, including all its contents, chapters, graphs, and examples, is provided for informational purposes only and should not be considered financial or investment advice. The ideas, concepts, and strategies presented are based on the author's experiences, observations, and opinions. They are not a recommendation to buy or sell any security or engage in any particular investment strategy.

Investing inherently carries risks, including the potential for loss of principal. The value of investments can go up and down, and past performance does not necessarily indicate future results. The strategies and examples in this book are no guarantee of future success.

It's essential to exercise due diligence and critically assess the applicability of any strategy or information to your situation. Financial markets, economic conditions, and personal situations change over time. As a result, an approach or idea that was effective at one point in time might not be appropriate later.

The author has made efforts to ensure the accuracy and relevance of the content at the time of publishing. However, due to the dynamic nature of financial markets and the potential for changes in regulations and laws, the content may not always be up to date, and the author does not provide any guarantees, warranties, or representations, either expressed or implied, regarding the accuracy, completeness, or applicability of any information contained within.

Under no circumstances shall the author, publisher, or any of their respective affiliates, partners, or associates be held liable for any direct, indirect, consequential, punitive, special, or any other damages arising from your reliance upon this book or for any decisions you make based on its content.

Readers should approach this book as a general guide rather than a definitive investment roadmap. Remember always to prioritize due diligence, remain aware of the risks, and seek out the insights and expertise of qualified experts if your circumstances warrant.

To Patricia

Acknowledgments

I am grateful to the many financial advisors and others who selflessly reviewed the manuscript of *Wealthier*. You can find their comments on the website for this book: https://wealthierbook.com/reviews-endorsements/

I especially benefitted from the wisdom of Sarah Charles, Linda Parks, and Brian Remson.

Rubin Miller, the founder of Peltoma Capital Partners, spent many hours reviewing the manuscript and conveying his insights to me. I couldn't be more grateful.

Larry Swedroe explained the nuances of alternatives that may be appropriate to those with larger portfolios. He is a prolific author and prominent thought leader, yet he is always generous in sharing his expertise.

I couldn't have written the chapter on life insurance without the patient guidance of Chuck Hinners.

Eddie O'Neal, Ph.D, reviewed the manuscript and gave me the invaluable benefit of his expertise, patiently fielding endless questions with grace and understanding.

I want to thank Bill Bernstein, author of several seminal financial books, for his kind review.

A special thanks to Knut Rostad and Ben Felix for doing the same.

I can't write books without the help of my author's assistant, Danielle Acee, or the line editors, endnote specialists, proofreaders, indexers, and many others who work behind the scenes to ensure a manuscript is as good as we can make it.

Given her contributions, my wife, Patricia, should be listed as co-author, but she declined. Fortunately, she didn't decline my offer many years ago to be my partner for life.

Daniel R. Solin
April 1, 2024

Contents

- 12 **Introduction**
  A Friend in Need
- 18 **Context Matters**

- 30 **Part One**
  Good Investing
- 32 **Chapter 1**
  Investing is Simple *and* Easy
- 40 **Chapter 2**
  The Factor Factor
- 43 **Chapter 3**
  Retirement Plan Investing
- 48 **Chapter 4**
  Socially Responsible Investing

- 52 **Part Two**
  Bad Investing
- 54 **Chapter 5**
  Alternative Investments
- 59 **Chapter 6**
  Lotto Luck?
- 61 **Chapter 7**
  Cryptocurrency Confusion
- 64 **Chapter 8**
  Investing Myths
- 71 **Chapter 9**
  Terrible Consequences

- 74 **Part Three**
  The Ugly Reality
- 76 **Chapter 10**
  Something Needs to Change
- 79 **Chapter 11**
  A Rigged System

- 84 **Part Four**
  Practice Stoic Finance
- 86 **Chapter 12**
  Letting Go
- 89 **Chapter 13**
  Perspective Power
- 94 **Chapter 14**
  Don't Look
- 97 **Chapter 15**
  Masterly Inactivity
- 100 **Chapter 16**
  Don't Be Intimidated
- 105 **Chapter 17**
  Ignore Naked Pundits
- 108 **Chapter 18**
  Don't Look for Patterns

- 112 **Part Five**
  DIY Financial Planning
- 114 **Chapter 19**
  Real Love

116	**Chapter 20** The Hype and the Reality	170	**Part Eight** **Securing Shelter**
119	**Chapter 21** Monte Carlo Analysis Can Be Misused	172	**Chapter 34** Buy or Rent?
122	**Chapter 22** Entrepreneurial Courage	177	**Chapter 35** To Prepay or Not to Prepay?
126	**Part Six** **Getting to "the Number"**	182	**Part Nine** **Beat Your Brain**
128	**Chapter 23** How Much is Enough?	184	**Chapter 36** Will Power
132	**Chapter 24** The Role of Gratitude	187	**Chapter 37** Don't Be a Stranger
136	**Chapter 25** A Trap for the Unwary	190	**Chapter 38** Brain Barriers
139	**Chapter 26** Smoothing Over Savings	192	**Part Ten** **Need Help?**
143	**Chapter 27** Modern Budgeting	194	**Chapter 39** Decoding Fees
145	**Chapter 28** Slay Student Loans	198	**Chapter 40** Cutting Costs
148	**Chapter 29** Tax Tricks	201	**Chapter 41** Studies that Quantify Value
151	**Chapter 30** Shortfalls	204	**Chapter 42** AI is Your New BFF
154	**Part Seven** **A Twist on Risk**	208	**Conclusion** **Trust Yourself**
156	**Chapter 31** Insurable Risks		
161	**Chapter 32** A Mind-blowing Life Insurance Secret	210	**Endnotes**
		220	**Resources**
		221	**AI Disclosure**
166	**Chapter 33** Uninsurable Risks	222	**Index**

Introduction:
A Friend in Need

> *Financial empowerment means that a person feels in control of their money. We found that people who feel empowered in their financial lives experience more joy, peace, satisfaction, and pride concerning their finances.*
> —Samantha Lamas, "What is Financial Empowerment and Why is it Important?," *Morningstar*

Decisions about how you save, spend, and invest your money can profoundly impact your future. I understand why you seek guidance, insights, and strategies to navigate this complex landscape. The future is uncertain, the idea of building wealth feels daunting. Financial experts provide conflicting advice, much of which seems unrelatable.

Why Listen to Me?

I'm not a financial advisor. You can't hire me. My only allegiance is to you. I have one goal: to provide the research-based advice you need to achieve financial freedom.

I wrote *The Smartest Investment Book You'll Ever Read* in 2006. I advised buying three index funds (where the fund manager replicates the performance of a market index) from Vanguard and ignoring Wall Street "experts."

My view then—and now—is that the goal of many of those who want to "help" you invest your money is to transfer wealth from your pocket to theirs.

That hasn't changed.

The premise in my *Smartest Investment* book, that you can do just as well—and likely better—on your own, was ridiculed by many in the brokerage community who believed that active mutual fund managers could outperform their benchmark indexes through stock picking and market timing.

And yet:

Smartest Investment was enthusiastically reviewed by the *NY Times*.
It is on Derek Sivers' list of recommended books.
Kiplinger's listed *Smartest Investment* as one of five classic investment books investors should read.

Style Rave listed *Smartest Investment* as one of nine "must-read financial books for every person of color."

I went on CNBC's *Power Lunch* in 2009 and said, "One of the things you could do is give us more 'In Bogle we Trust' and much less 'In Cramer we Trust.'" Cramer went ballistic, which remains an enduring source of pride.

Time has proved my approach right.

As of the end of 2023, index based funds (exchange-traded funds and notes and passively managed mutual funds) reached $13.29 trillion in assets, which was slightly *greater* than the $13.23 trillion held in actively managed funds.

What was considered controversial in 2006 is now mainstream.

I went on to write a series of *Smartest* investing books, to the great dismay of the securities industry. I've written thousands of blogs, appeared on many TV and radio programs, and was featured in prominent investing magazines.

I support the information in this book with extensive Endnotes. Please refer to them if you want more information on any subject.

Millennials Need Advice

Achieving wealth is more than managing your money; it's about controlling your life.

Being in control of your finances isn't that hard. I'll show you how.

If you identify as one of the roughly 97.5 million do-it-yourself (DIY) investors (primarily millennials) navigating your finances without an advisor, this book is a beacon of sound, no-nonsense wisdom.

The securities industry and financial media have done a great job misleading millennials and other investors.

It's unsurprising that millennials react "strongly and inconsistently" to stock market volatility by moving from stocks to savings and deposits when the stock market declines. One survey found working millennials held 33% of their retirement savings accounts in cash.

This behavior alone has serious adverse consequences for achieving long-term financial goals.

Millennials are also more inclined than other investors to be seduced by the allure of actively managed investments, which further erodes their long-term returns.

Millennials have more appetite for alternative investments like cryptocurrency and commodities. The evidence doesn't support this enthusiasm.

On average, millennials have the goal to retire at age 62. That won't happen without a dramatic shift in thinking.

The information in this book can change ingrained, harmful beliefs about investing and help you reach your goals.

Why DIY?

There are many reasons why you might opt to be a DIY investor. Perhaps you can't afford a financial advisor, or your assets don't meet their minimum requirements. Maybe you want to take sole responsibility for your financial life, or you don't trust the establishment or feel they don't understand your unique needs and goals.

Even if you want to use an advisor, you may have little choice but to deal with your finances alone. Most financial advisors don't want your business. They cater to high-net-worth investors with complex financial planning needs.

No-fuss DIY Investing

I'm going to show you how to invest in a way that's simple *and* easy.

There's no research involved. You don't have to pay any attention to what's going on with the stock market.
The less you do (after putting in the work to design a plan), the better your experience will be.

The securities industry (and social media) will bully you into believing you have to constantly work at investing. It wants to create fear and anxiety so you'll trade more and generate commissions *for them*. It wants to sell you complex, high-fee products because that's what's best for *its* bottom line.

It's now easier than ever to invest intelligently and responsibly.

You can invest in only *two* low-fee, exchange-traded funds and have a globally diversified portfolio in an asset allocation (the division of your portfolio between stocks, bonds, and cash) suitable for your unique requirements.

By adjusting the percentage of your portfolio allocated to stocks, you can increase or decrease the volatility and expected returns of this portfolio.

Because of the begrudging recognition that investing has been "commoditized" (meaning it's so easy anyone can do it), the new buzz phrase in the investment community is "comprehensive financial planning."

Don't be overwhelmed by the prospect of DIY financial planning. Following some basic guidelines, you can intelligently plan for your future.

Spotting Misinformation

You're bombarded by a tsunami of misinformation from the powerful securities industry, which seeks to undermine your efforts to use a simple, responsible, and intelligent investment strategy.

They work closely with their partners, the financial media, which features a steady diet of "pundits" opining on everything from the market's direction to the next hot mutual fund. They have no accountability. There's little credible evidence their views are based on anything other than rank speculation.

If that wasn't enough, your brain is a barrier to succeeding as a DIY investor. It's programmed to find patterns where none exist (see Chapter 18). It encourages you to procrastinate and fail to plan for your future (see Chapter 37).
It's worse if you have psychological biases that cause you to invest recklessly or impulsively. (see Chapters 6 and 13).

These forces combine to imperil your efforts to be financially responsible and reach your retirement goals. As a result, many give up or kick the can down the road.

I'll show you how to identify and overcome these obstacles.

Retaining a Financial Advisor

Before you dive into this book, I want to address a common question: Should you retain a financial advisor if you meet the minimum of some (but not all) advisors?

Retaining a financial advisor is prudent if you have significant assets or complex financial, tax, or estate planning issues. You'll need to determine if you are the right client and if they are the right advisor.

I'll provide the information you need to select the best financial advisor for your needs (see Chapters 39, 40, and 41).

A Counterintuitive Message

Most DIY investors have simple investing and financial planning needs. If you fit into this category, my message is counterintuitive: Both investing and basic financial planning are simple and easy.

My goal isn't to exhaustively set forth all the financial issues you're likely to confront. In the Resources section, I list some excellent books that cover the main subjects of this book in more detail.

My goal is to make you "wealthier" as a successful DIY investor and financial planner by providing insights you won't find elsewhere.

You've found a friend indeed.

Context Matters

Context constitutes 90 percent of a message, words only 10 percent.
—Abhijit Naskar, *Honor He Wrote: 100 Sonnets for Humans Not Vegetables*

Below are some key financial concepts and the context for how each fits into the fundamental principles discussed in this book.

Actively managed mutual fund

A mutual fund where the fund manager attempts to outperform the returns of a specific index, like the S&P 500®.

Context: You should avoid actively managed mutual funds. The evidence is compelling that most of them underperform index funds and exchange-traded funds (ETFs), especially over the long term and after fees and taxes.

Where is it discussed? Chapters 3 and 8.

Alternative investments

Investments that aren't traditional stocks, bonds, or cash. Examples include, hedge funds, cryptocurrency, commodities, and private equity.

Context*:* The returns frequently don't match the hype.

Where is it discussed? Chapter 5.

Amygdala

A region in the brain involved in processing emotions.

Context: Money is a very emotional subject. It's essential to understand how the brain processes emotions in order to make sound financial decisions. We like to think we are rational, but that's not always true.

"Amygdala hijack" occurs when a person's reaction to something is immediate and intense, bypassing rational thought. When markets tank, the emotional part of our brain dominates the rational part, leading to impulsive decisions.

Where is it discussed? Chapter 13.

Apophenia

Seeing patterns in random data.

Context: It's not entirely your fault that you see patterns where none exist. Your brain is predisposed to doing so. Be wary of conclusions drawn from these misperceived patterns.

Where is it discussed? Chapter 18.

Bear market

A market condition where prices of securities fall, generally by 20% or more from recent highs.

Context: Historically, bear markets are followed by bull markets. The key is not to panic.

Where is it discussed? Chapter 13.

Behavioral finance

A study that combines psychological theory with conventional economics to explain why people make irrational financial decisions.

Context: Most financial experts believe controlling your behavior is critical to becoming a successful investor. The key is to learn to control your own behavior rather than making impulsive, emotionally driven decisions.

Where is it discussed? Chapters 3, 14, 15, 18 and 41.

Benchmark

A standard against which the performance of a security or investment can be measured.

Context: When you read about outperforming actively managed funds, be aware that they often compare their "outperforming" results to an incorrect benchmark. For example, a large-capitalization U.S. stock mutual fund should be using the S&P 500 index as the correct benchmark.

Where is it discussed? Chapter 1.

Blended whole life insurance

A combination of term and whole life insurance which allows for both protection and cash-value accumulation.

Context: For some millennials, blended whole life insurance and universal life insurance may be worth considering if you can find an insurance agent who will discount commissions on these policies.

Where is it discussed? Chapter 32.

Bond

A debt security that certifies the borrower will repay the amount to the holder at a later date, typically with interest.

Context: Not all bonds are created equal. My investment recommendation is a bond fund that consists primarily of short-term Treasury bonds backed by the full faith and credit of the U.S. government, although there are situations where some investors should consider a longer term, higher yielding Treasury bond, assuming liquidity is not an issue.

Where is it discussed? Chapter 1.

Bull market

A market condition characterized by the rise in securities prices.

Context: Bull markets historically follow bear markets. No one can predict when. It often happens when least expected. Patient investors wait out bear markets to reap the benefits of bull markets.

Where is it discussed? Chapter 13.

Cocaine phone

A phone where you put addictive and time-consuming apps and information. When combined with a "kale phone," it can be an excellent way to increase productivity.

Where is it discussed? Chapter 37.

Compound interest

Interest is calculated on the initial amount as well as on the accumulated interest.

Context: The key to success as a millennial investor is benefitting from compound interest.

Where is it discussed? Chapter 26.

Cryptocurrency

A digital or virtual form of currency that uses cryptography for security.

Context: The reality doesn't live up to the hype. It's high risk, and mining associated with it harms the environment.

Where is it discussed? Chapter 7.

Diversification

Spreading investments among and within different asset classes (like stocks, bonds, and cash), industries, and geographic regions to reduce risk.

Context: A classic strategy for reducing the risk of an investment portfolio.

Where is it discussed? Chapter 1.

Dopamine

A neurotransmitter in the brain that affects emotions, movements, and sensations of pleasure.

Context: The brain craves dopamine. Knowing what triggers its release will help you understand how you react to financial issues.

Where is it discussed? Chapters 6 and 14.

Endowment effect

Valuing something more when we own it.

Context: When you understand this bias, you'll appreciate how it can influence your investing behavior in irrational and harmful ways.

Where is it discussed? Chapter 14.

Environmental, social, and governance-based (ESG) investing

ESG investing focuses on sustainable, responsible strategies.

Context: Commonly known as "socially responsible investing," ESG presents an opportunity to invest in a way that's true to your values, but you may have to sacrifice returns to do so.

Where is it discussed? Chapter 4.

Exchange-traded fund (ETF)

An investment fund traded on stock exchanges, much like stocks. Most ETFs are index funds.

Context: ETFs have significant benefits (like lower investment minimums and more control of the trading price) that may make them preferable to index mutual funds for some investors.

Where is it discussed? Chapters 1, 2 ,3, and 4.

Expected returns

The amount of profit or loss an investor can anticipate receiving on an investment.

Context: No one can predict actual returns, but using historical data (available from websites like *Yahoo Finance*) permits an estimate of future likely returns for stocks. For bonds, current yields are indicative of present and future returns, if they are held to maturity.

Where is it discussed? Chapters 1, 23, and 35.

Expense ratio

A yearly management fee charged by ETFs and mutual funds. It is expressed as a percentage of average assets under management.

Context: Mutual funds with the highest expense ratios tend to underperform those with lower expense ratios. Just because something costs more doesn't mean it's better.

Where is it discussed? Chapters 1, 3, 4, and 41.

Factor-based portfolio

An investment strategy where securities are chosen based on attributes commonly associated with higher returns. These attributes, known as factors, are identified through academic research as having a significant influence on a security's performance relative to the stock market. The most widely recognized factors include value, size, momentum, quality, and volatility.

Context: A factor-based portfolio may be a good option for younger investors who can tolerate lower returns and have the time and discipline to persist when their factor-based portfolio underperforms a market-cap-weighted portfolio.

Where is it discussed? Chapter 2.

Fee-only insurance consultants

Consultants who provide advice for a fee and don't sell insurance products.

Context: The best-kept secret in the insurance industry is the existence of these consultants who charge an hourly fee and provide insurance-related advice that is objective.

Where is it discussed? Chapter 32.

Financial planning

An ongoing process that looks at your entire financial picture to create strategies for achieving your short- and long-term goals.

Context: While helpful, financial planning has serious limitations. It often promises more than it delivers.

Where is it discussed? Chapters 12, 19, 20, 21, 25, 27, and 29.

Greenwashing

Deceptively marketing products as environmentally friendly.

Context: The mutual fund industry can take a good thing (socially responsible investing) and engage in unethical behavior to deceive investors.

Where is it discussed? Chapter 4.

Health Savings Account (HSA)

A tax-advantaged account for individuals with high-deductible health plans to save for medical expenses.

Context: HSAs are underutilized, tax-advantaged accounts that can help you deal with rising healthcare costs and medical expenses.

Where is it discussed? Chapters 27, 29, and 33.

Index fund

A mutual fund designed to track components of a market index.

Context: Index funds, passively managed funds, and ETFs are the keys to reaching your financial goals and maximizing your wealth with minimal effort.

Where is it discussed? Chapters 1, 3, and 8.

Information bias

The tendency to seek and evaluate information, even if it's irrelevant, to the issue at hand.

Context: Not all information is of equal importance. Investors suffer from too much information and not the lack of it.

Where is it discussed? Chapter 14.

Kale phone

A phone where you put only essential, useful apps and information. When combined with a "cocaine phone," it can be an excellent way to increase productivity.

Where is it discussed? Chapter 37.

Loss aversion

A cognitive bias where the pain of incurring losses is more powerful than the pleasure of positive returns.

Context: This bias can cause irrational investor behavior like seeking lottery-like returns.

Where is it discussed? Chapters 6 and 14.

Mandatory arbitration

A mandatory requirement to settle disputes through arbitration rather than the court system.

Context: Few investors understand that opening a brokerage account means giving up their constitutional right to a jury trial and subjecting themselves to arbitration administered by the Financial Industry Regulatory Authority (FINRA).
Where is it discussed? Chapter 11.

Market-cap weighted

Constructing a portfolio of investments or an index where individual components are included in proportions based on their market capitalization. Market capitalization, or market cap, is calculated by multiplying the current share price by the total number of outstanding shares. This figure gives the total market value of a company's equity. A market-cap weighted portfolio or index gives greater influence to larger companies.

Context: The simple and straightforward investing strategy outlined in Chapter 1 is market-cap weighted.

Where is it discussed? Chapter 2.

Masterly inactivity

A strategy of deliberate inactivity.

Context: Investing is one of the few activities in life where less activity is likely to generate superior results.

Where is it discussed? Chapter 15.

Monte Carlo analysis

A mathematical technique used to estimate possible outcomes of an uncertain event.

Context: It's easy to be seduced by the power of computerized analysis, but your reliance on a Monte Carlo analysis can be misplaced because it may not adequately account for real-world events.

Where is it discussed? Chapter 21.

Roth IRA

An individual retirement account allowing post-tax contributions with tax-free growth.

Context: An excellent way to save for retirement, but you must overcome the appeal of immediate tax benefits in exchange for tax-free withdrawals at age 59½ or older.

Where is it discussed? Chapters 3, 16, 29 and 35.

Stock

A type of security that represents ownership in a corporation and is a claim on part of the corporation's assets and earnings.

Context: Instead of trying to pick stock "winners," it's prudent to purchase an index fund, ETF, or a passively managed fund that holds a globally diversified portfolio of stocks.

Where is it discussed? Chapter 8.

Taxable brokerage account

An investment account that permits investors to use after-tax dollars to buy different investments.

Context: Benefits of taxable brokerage accounts include favorable tax treatment of profits and lack of restrictions.

Where is it discussed? Chapters 3 and 16.

Term life insurance

Life insurance that pays a benefit in the event of the insured's death during a specified term.

Context: If you can only afford the relatively inexpensive premiums for term insurance, it's better than no insurance.

Where is it discussed? Chapter 32.

Traditional IRA

An individual retirement account allowing pre-tax contributions. The growth of the account is taxed upon withdrawal. The IRS refers to these accounts as "Individual Retirement Arrangements," but they are more commonly known as "Individual Retirement Accounts."

Context: Traditional IRAs can play an important role in reaching your retirement goals, but you will pay tax on the total amount of withdrawals at your marginal tax rate when you reach 59½ or older, and no one knows what that tax rate will be.

Where is it discussed? Chapters 3 and 16.

Treasury Bills

Short-term government securities with a maturity of one year or less.

Context: The purpose of your bond portfolio is to mitigate volatility, not generate returns. Treasury Bills are backed by the full faith and credit of the U.S. government and are excellent for this purpose.

Where is it discussed? Chapter 1.

Universal life insurance

A type of permanent life insurance with a cash value component and flexible premium payments.

Context: While these policies are more expensive than term policies, it's possible to negotiate commissions on blended whole life and universal life insurance from certain carriers, making these policies attractive for some individuals.

Where is it discussed? Chapter 32.

Notes

Part One
Good Investing

Do this.

Chapter 1
Investing *is* Simple and Easy

> *Would you believe me if I told you that there's an investment strategy that a seven-year-old could understand, will take you fifteen minutes of work per year, outperform 90 percent of finance professionals in the long run, and make you a millionaire over time?*
> —William J. Bernstein, If You Can: How Millennials Can Get Rich Slowly

The system isn't working for most Americans, largely because it's rigged against small investors (discussed in Chapters 10 and 11).

For those who need no convincing and just want to know how to invest to maximize the possibility of reaching your financial goals, here's the information you need to know.

Warren Buffett said, "Investing is simple but not easy." If you have the correct information, it's both simple *and* easy to implement. It still can be challenging to ignore the formidable forces (including your brain) aligned against you that encourage bad investor behavior.

William J. Bernstein is one of the most respected financial authors in the U.S. Two of his books, *The Four Pillars of Investing* and *The Intelligent Asset Allocator,* are investment classics.

What was the remarkable investment strategy he recommended referenced in the chapter quote? Buy three low-fee index funds for your portfolio of stocks and bonds.

My suggestion is even less complex: Buy two exchange-traded funds (ETFs).

What's an ETF?

An ETF operates like a mutual fund. It typically holds a basket of stocks or bonds that track a benchmark index. Some ETFs hold commodities.

They are called "exchange-traded funds" because they are "funds" that hold a collection of stocks, bonds, or other securities that are "traded" on stock "exchanges."

ETFs vs Index Mutual Funds

While index mutual funds and ETFs have many similarities, a primary difference is how they trade. ETFs trade just like stocks. When the market is open, you can buy and sell them. Index funds can be purchased only after the markets close (although you can place an order to buy or sell them at any time).

Because of this difference, the price of ETFs fluctuates throughout the trading day. The price of an index fund changes only once a day.

This difference isn't an advantage of ETFs over index mutual funds in the long term because it's unlikely you will need to trade an ETF or an index mutual fund more than once a day.

Index mutual funds often have minimum investment requirements. ETFs have no minimums.

ETFs are more tax efficient than index funds because you often don't incur capital gains tax when the holdings in your ETF generate a profit, although you do incur taxes if you earn a profit on the sale of your ETFs. The amount of those taxes depends on the length of time you have held them.

Bogle's Advice

John Bogle was a titan of the investment world, best known for founding The Vanguard Group in 1974 and creating the first index mutual fund for individual investors. His low-cost index fund investing philosophy has earned him a place in the pantheon of investing legends.

Bogle was a fierce advocate for individual investors. He promoted a long-term, disciplined approach, focusing on minimizing fees and maximizing simplicity.

He emphasized the futility of trying to outperform the stock market through speculative trading.

This sage advice from Bogle should be framed and prominently displayed in your home: "In investing, you get what you *don't* pay for. Costs matter. So intelligent investors will use low-cost index funds to build a diversified portfolio of stocks and bonds, and they will stay the course. And they won't be foolish enough to think they can consistently outsmart the market."

Hundreds of articles in peer-reviewed journals support Bogle's wisdom. His advice applies whether you implement it with ETFs or index funds.

Why Invest in the Entire Stock Market?

Imagine you're in a giant candy store with just a few dollars to spend. You can either try to pick the best-looking candy bar and hope it tastes great, or you can buy a little piece of every single candy in the store so you're guaranteed to have some of the best candies, even if you also get some you don't like as much.

Buying the entire stock market is like buying a piece of every candy—you get a little bit of everything, but you are assured of getting some great-tasting candy.

What are Short-term U.S. Treasuries?

In investing, it's important to have a mix of growth (stocks) and safety (bonds).

Think of the stock market as a roller coaster. Stocks make the ride bumpier. Bonds help make your ride smoother.

Short-term U.S. Treasury Bills are stabilizers of your portfolio. Since they're due to be paid back soon, their value doesn't bounce around as much as stocks or long-term bonds. They add a nice, steady weight to your investment through the ups and downs of the market.

An ETF of short-term U.S. Treasuries offers a safe and stable component to your investment portfolio. Because they hold a basket of Treasuries with different maturity dates (typically ranging from one to three years) they manage interest rate risk better than holding Treasuries with only one maturity date. They are very liquid because you can buy and sell them at the market price whenever the stock market is open. Treasury Bills are typically held until maturity, although they can be sold before maturity at the market rate.

Short-term U.S. Treasuries are like IOUs from the U.S. government. When you buy them, you're basically lending money to the government. It promises to pay you back at the maturity date. Because they're guaranteed by the full faith and credit of the U.S. government, they're considered very safe.

The U.S. has issued debt since 1790. It has never defaulted.

Stocks: Risk vs. Reward

Buying individual stocks can lead to big wins, but it also comes with the chance of significant losses. Purchasing an ETF spreads your risk, so even if some stocks don't do well, others might do great, balancing things out.

Choosing individual stocks is like reading every candy wrapper in the store before deciding what to buy—it takes a lot of time, and you might still make the wrong choice.

An ETF that tracks an index is a quick pick. It's managed by professionals whose sole focus is to replicate the returns of the benchmark index less low management fees. You have more time to engage in activities you enjoy.

The Bottom Line

Investing in the entire stock market is about playing the long game—like planting a garden. You wouldn't just plant one type of flower and hope for the best. You'd plant many different kinds, knowing that even if some don't bloom, others will.

The stock market is the same. It might have ups and downs, but the entire market tends to grow over time.

Buying an ETF that tracks the whole market might not be as exciting as picking stocks, but it can lead to steady progress towards meeting your financial goals.

My recommended approach to investing is based on the premise that capturing the returns of two broad indexes (a global stock index and an index of U.S. Treasuries) is a simple, responsible, and intelligent way to invest long-term.

Who Agrees?

In addition to the wealth of data supporting this approach, here's a sampling of quotes from highly respected authors, investors, and others who agree:

> *A low-cost index fund is the most sensible equity investment for most investors.*
> —Warren Buffett, a legendary investor and the chairman of Berkshire Hathaway, renowned for his value-investing approach and for turning a failing textile mill into a colossal conglomerate, making him one of the wealthiest individuals in the world.

> *The public would be better off in an index fund.*
> —Peter Lynch, a celebrated investment author who was the former manager of the Magellan Fund at Fidelity Investments, where he averaged a 29.2% annual return from 1977 to 1990.

> *Experience conclusively shows that index-fund buyers will likely obtain results exceeding those of the typical fund manager, whose hefty advisory fees and substantial portfolio turnover tend to reduce investment yields.*
> —Burton Malkiel, a Princeton economist and the author of *A Random Walk Down Wall Street*.

> *Wall Street, with its army of brokers, analysts, and advisers funneling trillions of dollars into mutual funds, hedge funds, and private equity funds, is an elaborate fraud.*
> —Michael Lewis, author of bestsellers like Liar's Poker and The Big Short.

A survey of world-class economists, which included several Nobel Prize winners, unanimously agreed with the following statement: *In general, absent any inside information, an equity investor can expect to do better by holding a well-diversified, low-fee, passive index fund than by holding a few stocks.*

The Plan

My recommendations include a stock ETF that gives you exposure to the global stock market and a bond ETF that will provide stability to your portfolio when the stock market tanks.

Start with an understanding of two benchmark indexes.

> **1. The FTSE Global All Cap Index** covers both well-established and still-developing markets. For the period from January 2014 to January 2024, the annualized average return of the FTSE Global All Cap Index index was 8.31% per year. Returns for a longer period were not publicly available.

You can't buy the index, but you can access its returns through ETFs, like Vanguard's Total World Stock ETF, which invests in 9823 stocks, both foreign and domestic, in well-established and still-developing markets. The expense ratio (management fee) of VT is only 0.07%. As of January 31, 2024, VT had $43.5 billion under management.

> **2. The ICE BofA Merrill Lynch 1-3 Year U.S. Treasury Index:** This index tracks the performance of U.S. Treasury securities with maturities ranging from one to three years. It is a widely recognized benchmark for short-term U.S. Treasury bonds. For the period December 31, 1987 to December 29, 2023, the annualized average return of the ICE BofA Merrill Lynch 1-3 Year U.S. Treasury index was 4.93% per year.

One example of an ETF that aims to replicate this index is iShares 1-3 year Treasury Bond ETF (SHY). The expense ratio (management fee) of SHY is 0.15%. As of February 16, 2024, SHY had over $25 billion under management.

Note: Whether you invest in an index fund or an ETF, there can be slight differences in performance due to "tracking error" which refers to the divergence between the fund's performance and the index it tracks. This can occur due to management fees, trading costs, and imperfect index composition replication.

What About Foreign Bonds?

You may have noticed that the stock portion of your portfolio includes exposure to foreign stocks, but the bond portion is limited to U.S. Treasuries. Do you need to diversify your bond holdings to include foreign bonds?

The purpose of holding U.S. Treasuries is to mitigate the volatility of your portfolio. It isn't to increase returns. To increase expected returns, increase your allocation to stocks.

While some financial experts believe you don't need further diversification by gaining exposure to foreign bonds, others disagree.

Vanguard recommends a 30% allocation of your bond portfolio to international bonds. You may not need to follow this recommendation if your portfolio is small and uncomplicated.

You can quickly gain exposure to an index composed of non-U.S. developed market government bonds by investing in IGOV, an ETF that tracks that index. IGOV holds bonds from different countries, except for the U.S. When you invest in it, you are buying a small piece of many foreign government bonds at once. Its expense ratio is 0.35%.

Exposure to Stocks Impacts Expected Returns

The percentage of your portfolio allocated to stocks impacts your expected returns over time because stocks have traditionally earned more than bonds. The higher your allocation to stocks, the higher your expected returns will be, but your portfolio will be more volatile than one with a higher allocation to bonds.

Don't confuse "risk" with "volatility".

"Volatility" describes the change in the price of a security or an index (either up or down). Big changes in volatility can be stomach-churning, but they will only impact returns if you buy or sell.

"Risk" is described by *Morningstar* as "the possibility that you will not be able to meet your financial goals or honour your obligations, or that you will have to rethink your goals because circumstances have changed."

For younger investors, holding cash or low interest bearing bonds would be a risky portfolio if it didn't keep pace with inflation, but it wouldn't be volatile.

Common Allocations

While there are many possibilities for allocating your portfolio between stocks and bonds, here are common allocations:

20% stocks / 80% bonds (very conservative)
40% stocks / 60% bonds (conservative)
60% stocks / 40% bonds (growth-oriented)
80% stocks / 20% bonds (aggressive)

Most younger investors should allocate a higher percentage of their portfolios to stocks.

There is no one-size-fits-all approach to asset allocation. Different investors have different goals, risk tolerances, and time horizons.

You can customize your asset allocation by using an asset allocation calculator. The Vanguard and IPERS (Iowa Public Retirement System) websites have good ones.

Now you know how to be a responsible DIY investor.

Simple, right?

Wealthier Tip

Don't get caught up in trying to pick the right stocks. Stick with a reliable ETF that tracks a broad index.

Chapter 2
The Factor Factor

> *Investors who cannot tolerate periods of underperforming the market should not deviate from the market portfolio because they may engage in panicked selling after a period of poor performance, just when expected future returns are greatest, as relative valuations are cheapest.*
> —Larry Swedroe, "Factor Investing and its (Behavioral) Persistence: Facts and Fiction about the Zoo of Factors," *Kitces*

The investment strategy recommended in Chapter 1 for the stock portion of your portfolio is market-capitalization ("market cap") weighted.

What does this mean?

The "market cap" tells how big or small each company is. It's calculated by multiplying the number of their stock shares by the current price of each share. A big company with lots of shares and a high stock price will have a high market cap, while a smaller company will have a lower one.

For most investors, having a portfolio of stocks based on market-cap indexes is all they will need to achieve their financial goals.

However, you should know there's another way to invest, which is easily accessible to DIY investors: factor-based investing.

What is Factor-based Investing?

Factor-based investing is a strategy of investing in securities that have specific characteristics in an effort to achieve outperformance. It's based on extensive research demonstrating that stocks with these characteristics may outperform other stocks over long periods of time.

Here are a few common factors:

- **Size:** Smaller companies can grow quickly
- **Value:** Stocks that are a good deal based on their long-term projections
- **Momentum:** A company that's been doing well recently
- **Quality:** Strong companies that make good profits
- **Volatility:** How much the stock's price goes up and down

Proponents of factor-based investing "tilt" portfolios toward stocks with these factors. They believe doing so will achieve higher returns than a traditional market-cap-weighted portfolio.

Factor-based Investing vs Market-Cap-Weighted Investing

Market-cap investing is simple and easy to understand. It tends to be more resilient when the market tanks and offers more consistent returns.

Factor-based investing offers the potential for higher returns over the long term, but there can be long periods when it underperforms a comparable market-cap-based portfolio. The potential for higher returns with factor-based portfolios means taking more risk and experiencing higher volatility.

If you are a more conservative investor seeking steady returns and low volatility, stick with the market-cap recommendations in Chapter 1.

If you are comfortable trading additional risk for the possibility of enhanced returns, and can cope with long periods of underperformance, I will show you the "simple and easy" way to become a factor-based investor.

Multifactor ETFs

For the stock portion of your portfolio, instead of investing in VT (recommended in Chapter 1), which is market-cap weighted, consider a "multifactor" ETF like Goldman Sachs ActiveBeta U.S. Large Cap Equity ETF (GSLC). It has a low expense ratio of only 0.09%. It tilts its portfolio toward value, momentum, high quality and low volatility stocks. It manages $11.49 billion in assets.

For the bond portion of your portfolio, you would still use SHY or a similar ETF that invests primarily in short-term Treasury Bills.

That's it.

You're now a factor-based investor.

Wealthier Tip

For investors willing to trade more volatility for potentially higher returns, consider factor-based investing.

Chapter 3
Retirement Plan Investing

Most plans in the analysis had exclusively, or a substantial majority, actively managed funds. These are significantly more expensive than index funds and may also deliver a portion of their revenue to the providers or brokers (in a practice known as "revenue sharing").
—Americas Best 401(k), "Fees Run High for Small Business Run 401(k) Plans"

If you're employed, your employer likely sponsors a retirement plan (more for freelancers and entrepreneurs later in the chapter). The most common plans are 401(k), 403(b), and 457(b).

- **401(k)** plans allow employees to contribute a portion of their pre-tax income toward retirement savings. These contributions are invested and grow tax-deferred until retirement age.
- **403(b)** plans are similar to 401(k) plans but are offered by nonprofit organizations like schools and hospitals.
- **457(b)** plans are offered to government employees, allowing for pre-tax contributions toward retirement savings.

Many employers offer matching contributions for retirement plan participants.

A typical matching formula is for the company to match 50% of the first 6% of an employee's salary contribution. If an employee earns $50,000 and contributes $3,000 to her retirement plan, the employer would "match" by contributing $1,500. These contributions add "free money" to retirement savings.

The specifics of how matching contributions work vary depending on the employer's plan and policy.

Expensive options: The overwhelming majority of retirement plans in the U.S. are sponsored by small businesses with under 100 employees.

Many of these plans have limited, expensive investment options. Employees lose what would otherwise be contributed to their plan in fees.

No less an authority than Morningstar has observed: "If you've been following Morningstar's research for long, you know how important we think the cost of investing is. The expense ratio is the most proven predictor of future fund returns—and our data agrees."

One study found fees can cost a median-income, two-earner family nearly $155,000 and consume almost one-third of total investment returns over a lifetime. A higher-income, dual-earner household can lose as much as $277,969.

The management fee ("expense ratio") for mutual funds in plans offered by the largest platforms used by small businesses ranged from 1.19% to 1.95%.

Compare these exorbitant fees to the ETFs recommended in Chapter 1:

ETF	Expense ratio
VT	0.07%
SHY	0.15%

This difference in expense ratios is meaningful over the long term.

Expense ratios aren't the only fees embedded into retirement plans. Other fees include administrative, marketing, management, and trading costs.

Poor investment choices: Most of the small business plans in one comprehensive study had limited or no access to index funds. Instead, the investment options were populated with more expensive, actively managed funds.

These funds are likely to underperform lower-cost, comparable index funds, as explained in Chapter 8.

Employers who genuinely care about their employees are fighting back. They seek providers who will include low-cost index funds in their plan and deliver an all-in cost between 0.55% and 0.75% annually, including custody and recordkeeping fees and advisory services.

How You Should Invest Your Retirement Savings

Investing in a 401(k) plan (and other retirement plans) with limited investment options and high expense ratios can take time and effort. However, you can still employ strategies to improve a bad situation.

Maximize employer match: If your employer offers a match, contribute enough to get the maximum match. This is free money that can significantly boost your retirement savings.

If your employer doesn't match and the investment options are poor or expensive (or both), don't invest in the plan. You have many alternatives, including:

> **A traditional (pre-tax) Individual Retirement Account (IRA)**
> **A Roth (after-tax) Individual Retirement Account (if you qualify)**
> **A Health Savings Account**
> **A taxable brokerage account**

Diversify within limitations. Even with the limited options in retirement plans, diversify your investments across different asset classes (e.g., stocks, bonds, and cash). Look for funds that cover various sectors and regions to spread the risk.

Choose lower-cost funds. Select funds with the lowest expense ratios among the available investment options. If one of the options in your plan is a target retirement fund from a well-known fund manager like Vanguard, Fidelity, or Schwab, consider investing all your contributions in that fund, assuming the expense ratio is 0.50% or lower and the asset allocation in the fund is suitable.

Target date funds have a mix of stocks and bonds in a single fund. They adjust the allocation automatically to take more risk when you are young and become more conservative as you near retirement. They are as close to "autopilot" as you can get with an investment.

If that's not an option, look for low-cost index funds or ETFs that track a broad domestic benchmark (like the Wilshire 5000 Total Market Index), a broad international stock benchmark (like the FTSE Global All Cap Index), and a short-term bond index (like the ICE BofA Merrill Lynch 1–3 Year U.S. Treasury Index). Allocate your contributions between those funds in a suitable asset allocation.

If you have many years until retirement, you can tolerate high volatility and allocate more heavily to stocks.

Advocate for better options. Talk to your employer or HR department about the limited choices and high expense ratios of the investment options in your retirement plan. They may be willing to consider better choices.

Freelancers and Entrepreneurs

The road to retirement can seem fraught with uncertainty for freelancers and entrepreneurs. Without the cushion of employer-sponsored retirement plans, like 401(k)s, you need to navigate retirement planning on your own.

Freelancers and entrepreneurs face a unique set of obstacles. They often have irregular income. They don't have employers withholding money for taxes and health insurance, and they don't have an employer matching their retirement contributions. These factors make careful budgeting and planning all the more important.

Fortunately, there are excellent retirement plan options for freelancers and entrepreneurs that you can easily implement. Contribution limits and other requirements change annually.

Here are the most popular ones:

- **Traditional IRA:** Contributions are tax deductible, but you'll pay taxes at your marginal rate when you withdraw in retirement.
- **Roth IRA:** Contributions are made with after-tax dollars but grow tax-free, and withdrawals are tax- free in retirement. There are income limitations to qualify for Roth IRAs, so check to be sure your modified adjusted gross income doesn't exceed the maximum permitted.
- **Solo 401(k):** A Solo 401(k) is designed for self-employed individuals without employees. It allows you to contribute as both the employer and the employee, significantly increasing the potential contribution limit, which can be substantial (a total of $69,000 in 2024, with an

- additional contribution of $7,500 for those 50 or older).
- **Simplified Employee Pension Plan (SEP IRA):** A SEP IRA allows you to contribute a percentage of your income, capped at a limit that changes annually. This plan is easier to set up than a Solo 401(k), but the Solo 401(k) may offer more flexibility and higher contributions.
- **Savings Incentive Match Plan for Employees (SIMPLE IRA):** A SIMPLE IRA plan provides small employers with a simplified method to contribute toward their employees' and their own retirement savings. Employees may choose to make salary reduction contributions, and the employer must make matching or nonelective contributions. Contributions are made to an Individual Retirement Account or Annuity (IRA) set up for each employee (a SIMPLE IRA).
- **Health Savings Account (HSA):** An HSA can double as a retirement-savings tool if you have a high-deductible health plan. Funds can be used tax free for medical expenses and after age 65 for any purpose without penalty (though you'll pay income tax if not used for medical expenses).

If you combine these retirement plans with saving for retirement in a non-retirement, after-tax account, following the strategies in Chapters 1 or 2, you should be well on your way to funding a successful retirement.

Wealthier Tip

Company retirement plans are often filled with overpriced, underperforming investment options, so choose carefully. If you're a freelancer or entrepreneur, you have several attractive options.

Chapter 4
Socially Responsible Investing

> *ESG investing is a process that focuses on long-term risks ignored by classic Wall Street analysis. Think climate change, natural resource scarcity, or a toxic management culture that won't allow a company to compete for the most talented workers.*
> —Blaine Townsend, "What is ESG Investing?," Fortune Recommends

Younger investors are leading the way with socially responsible investing. They have high levels of engagement with climate change. A stunning 90% of millennials are interested in pursuing sustainable investments.

One survey found that 82% of Gen Z and nearly two-thirds of young millennial investors "have exposure" to environmental, social, and governance (ESG) investments.

What is Socially Responsible Investing?

Socially responsible investing is an approach to investing that considers financial returns and social and environmental impact. It involves investing in companies that align with personal values and ethics like those that prioritize sustainability, diversity and inclusion, and ethical business practices.

There are many options for socially responsible investing. More than 550 ESG mutual funds and ETFs were available to U.S. investors by mid-2022, with assets near $300 billion.

If you are considering investing in an ESG fund, you want to be sure the fund matches your investment goals, objectives, risk tolerance, and preferences.

The SEC notes that there is no standard definition of what constitutes "environmental, social and governance." How these terms are implemented can differ widely depending on the fund. Some funds may focus on ESG investing while others consider more traditional factors, like growth or value. How funds interpret terms like "governance" can vary. Does it mean shareholder's rights, diversity, or both?

Check to see if your fund relies on data from a third-party provider to "score" its investments. This information could be subjective or unreliable. Different providers could weigh ESG criteria differently.

The securities industry is keen to capitalize on emerging trends. Being honest and straightforward does not always guide its business practices.

Beware of "greenwashing."

"Greenwashing" refers to marketing a fund as environmentally sensitive but not implementing sustainability practices. As stated by Nasdaq, "Simply put, much of what passes as ESG is more sizzle than steak or more marketing mush than substantive sustainability."

The SEC has cracked down on greenwashing by adopting a new rule requiring 80% of a fund's portfolio to match the description in its name.

One way to evaluate the impact of your ETF is to ask for an impact report. According to Jon Hale, Global Head of Sustainability Research at Morningstar, an impact report "...will give you a way to assess the impact of a fund as an investment. Impact reports talk about things like shareholder engagement, or the portfolio's carbon footprint or gender diversity on the Boards of the companies held. That's a good way to gain a sense of what impact you're having as an investor."

You can request an impact report from the fund managers. Contact the fund manager's customer support or investor relations department.

Returns of ESG Funds

Do you have to sacrifice returns to be a socially responsible investor? To answer this question, it's helpful to compare the returns of a popular ESG index to the S&P 500 since that is a commonly used benchmark.

The comparable ESG index is the S&P 500 ESG index. There's only limited data available because this index was created in April 2019. From its launch until the end of 2022, the S&P 500 ESG index outperformed the S&P 500 index by a cumulative 9.16%.

This isn't necessarily good news. The S&P 500 ESG index could just as likely underperform the S&P 500 index by that amount or more in the future.

There's support for the view that, among other factors, ESG investors are willing to pay more for those stocks, which lowers their cost of capital and also lowers expected returns.

A survey conducted by Stanford University found younger investors are willing to sacrifice moderate or even significant returns to bring about environmental, social, and governance changes.

If you aren't willing to risk lower returns by investing in ESG stocks, consider making a direct donation to selected charities instead.

How to Select an ESG ETF

Your initial concern should be whether the fund is aligned with your values. You can find ETFs that address various ESG issues, like climate change, natural resource management, pollution reduction, human rights, corporate governance, community relations, supply change sustainability, and many others.

Consider how adding an ESG ETF will impact your overall portfolio. Will it cause you to be overweighted in a particular industry or asset class? Will it reduce your global diversification? How will it affect the risk of your portfolio?

Look for ETFs that track an index for all the reasons outlined in Chapter 1. These funds will likely outperform actively managed funds that seek to beat the index's returns.

Focus on the management fees charged by the ETF. You'll find that funds seeking to replicate an index's returns generally charge lower management fees than their actively managed counterparts.

Here are suggestions to get you started, limited to large, well-established fund families and ETFs with low expense ratios. If these funds align with your values and fit into your portfolio, they would be solid choices.

> **Vanguard ESG U.S. Stock ETF (ESGV):** Tracks the FTSE US All Cap Choice Index, including large and small-capitalization stocks.

It excludes stocks of companies engaged in adult entertainment, alcohol, tobacco, cannabis, gambling, chemical and biological weapons, cluster munitions, anti-personnel landmines, nuclear weapons, conventional military weapons, civilian firearms, nuclear power, and coal, oil, and gas and those that do not meet specific labor, human rights, environmental, and anti-corruption standards as defined by the UN Global Compact Principles. It also excludes companies that don't meet particular diversity criteria. It has a low expense ratio of 0.09% and holds 1,480 stocks, which makes it quite diversified. As of August 31, 2023, it had $6.8 billion in assets under management.

> **iShares ESG Aware MSCI USA ETF (ESGU):** Tracks the MSCI USA Extended ESG Index composed of U.S. companies with positive environmental, social, and governance characteristics. It invests in large- and mid-cap U.S. stocks.

It screens out companies involved in civilian firearms, controversial weapons, tobacco, thermal coal, and oil sands. It holds 299 stocks and has an expense ratio of 0.15%. As of October 6, 2023, the fund had assets of $12,147,690,620, making it one of the largest ESG ETFs.

> **Vanguard ESG International Stock ETF (VSGX):** Tracks the FTSE Global All Cap ex US Choice Index, providing international exposure to large-, mid-, and small-capitalization stocks.

It excludes companies involved with adult entertainment, alcoholic beverages, tobacco products, cannabis cultivation, gambling, chemical or biological weapons, munitions, nuclear and other weapons, nuclear energy, coal, oil, and gas, or that fail to meet specific diversity criteria. It is broadly diversified, holding 5,873 stocks as of August 31, 2023. It has a low expense ratio of 0.12%. As of August 31, 2023, it had $3.4 billion under management.

Wealthier Tip

Since most of the ESG ETFs are newer, they don't have long-term track records, but if socially responsible investing is important to you, there are options worth considering.

52

Part Two
Bad Investing

Don't do this.

Chapter 5
Alternative Investments

[Alternative investments] promised to accomplish what bonds could not. They failed. I see no reason why the future will bring a different result.
—John Rekenthaler, "Alternative Investments have been Useless Since 2007," TEBI

The interest in alternatives to the stock market is understandable. Investors are nervous about stock market volatility and market downturns. Proponents of alternative investments believe they can add inflation protection, increase returns, lower volatility and add diversification benefits.

Examples of alternative investments often touted in the media include NFTs, art, collectibles, real estate, hedge funds and private equity. Recently, fractional ownership of these assets has gained popularity, especially with millennials.

High net-worth investors are the target market for alternatives. They had an average allocation of 9% of their portfolio to alternatives in 2022.

Most DIY investors don't have to be concerned with investing in alternatives. The investment strategy outlined in Chapter 1 should be adequate for your needs. If you have no interest in alternatives, you can move on to the next chapter.

Sobering Returns

John Rekenthaler at Morningstar looked at the overall returns of publicly traded alternatives in portfolios from February 2007 to January 2022.

Only one of the nine investment alternatives outperformed an intermediate bond fund, and that alternative (real estate) was significantly more volatile than the bond fund.

He also found the much-touted diversification benefit was less than advertised.

What are Fractional Investments?

Fractional investing refers to purchasing a part of a larger asset. Investors can own a share of something, like a piece of artwork, a parcel of real estate, or a share of stock, without buying the entire asset outright.

The fractional investment market has seen significant growth in recent years, driven by technology and the entry of new platforms that allow for the fractional ownership of a wide range of assets.

Some of the most common fractional investments, and their benefits and drawbacks, include:

Nonfungible Tokens (NFTs): Examples of NFTs include one-of-a-kind digital artwork, a rare virtual item in a video game, music, movies, and graphics. These assets can be bought and sold like traditional collectibles. They are stored on the blockchain and easily verifiable.

The primary benefit of NFTs is market efficiency. Cryptonews states, "Converting a physical product to a digital asset has the potential to improve supply chains, reduce intermediaries, and increase security."

Digitizing an asset can increase its value by permitting it to be broken up into fractions, which would otherwise be impossible for assets like jewelry and sculptures.

The blockchain technology that preserves information about NFTs is secure and reliable. NFTs can also reduce the volatility of a portfolio because its price is unlikely to correlate to stocks and bonds.

However, NFTs are volatile and illiquid, with limited buyers and sellers. They don't generate revenue. An investment in an NFT is premised on appreciation, which is uncertain.

NFTs are subject to fraud when the underlying asset is sold as an NFT without the permission of the creator of the work. NFT mining has a similar adverse impact on the environment as cryptocurrency (discussed in Chapter 7).

Art: The market for fractional art investing is growing rapidly. Masterworks, one of the leading platforms in this niche, reported 811,803 members and $882,509,470 in assets under management, as of September 12, 2023.

While art can generate high returns, investing in it is risky. It can be challenging to determine value, which can vary based on many different (and often unknowable) factors. Fees and costs to buy and sell can be significant.

Determining authenticity from fakes can be difficult and expensive. This observation on the website of Mariana Custodio, an online contemporary art gallery, is sobering, "The opaque and rather unregulated art market is actually, pretty vulnerable to forgeries, tax fraud, and money laundering—just to name a few."

Collectibles: This category can include vintage cars, sports memorabilia, wine and whiskey, comic books, sneakers, watches, jewelry, and designer handbags.

The market size for fractional collectibles is also growing, with platforms like Rally and Otis gaining popularity.

Collectibles can be difficult to understand, have high transaction costs, and may be counterfeit. The returns of collectibles may correlate with the performance of the greater financial market "as a better overall market often leads to a better collectible market."

Real estate: The global real estate market is vast, and fractional ownership represents a growing segment. Fundrise, a popular platform for fractional real estate investing, reports over two million users have used it to invest in real estate, venture capital, and private credit.

If you own a home, you already have a significant portion of your net worth in a real estate investment. If you have a globally diversified portfolio of stocks (like VT, recommended in Chapter 1), a small portion of your portfolio is invested in real estate.

There are many benefits to investing in real estate, either by owning it outright or purchasing a fractional interest, which includes potential appreciation of property, possible positive cash flow, increase in equity over time, tax benefits, potential protection against inflation, and diversification of your portfolio.

A major downside of real estate is the lack of liquidity. It can be challenging to dispose of physical real estate quickly.

High cash requirements can be another negative. Banks may insist on a large down payment, depending on the property type and location and your financial situation.

If you decide to invest in rental properties and manage them yourself, plan on spending time dealing with tenants and maintenance issues. If you are fine with doing that, owning rental properties can be an excellent way to accumulate wealth over time, while providing meaningful tax benefits.

A fractional investment in real estate eliminates the high cash and maintenance requirements, but the liquidity issue remains.

Stock market: Fractional shares in the stock market have become increasingly common. The most prominent platform, Robinhood, offers commission-free trading for stocks, ETFs, options, and cryptocurrencies. Fractional shares can be as small as 1/1,000,000 of a share.

As of August 2023, Robinhood reported 23.2 million net cumulative-funded accounts and net revenues of $486 million.

Intellectual property and media: Fractional shares can be bought in creative works and digital properties including music, film, or television royalties.

MusicSplit permits you to buy fractions of songs. Songvest focuses on music royalties. Royalty Exchange auctions the rights to royalties on music, movies, and other properties. Publica is a "borderless peer-to-peer publishing platform where authors upload a book, and buyers purchase tradeable tokens in the book to trade or gift to others."

Should You Invest?

The proliferation of fractional investment opportunities reflects a broader trend toward increased accessibility and democratization of wealth-building tools.

While this may be a positive development, fractional investments have the following risks, which should be carefully evaluated:

- **Limited control:** Investors typically have little to no say in the management or the decision-making process related to the asset.
- **Limited liquidity:** While some fractional investments offer liquidity, others, like real estate, art, and collectibles may have periods where cashing out is not easy, immediate, or straightforward.
- **Fees:** Fees can be associated with the platforms facilitating these investments, which can eat into profits.
- **Platform risk:** Platforms facilitating these investments may not be financially stable or even honest, which can cause a meaningful loss of your investment.
- **Market risk:** Fractional ownership does not eliminate the inherent risks of investing. If the asset depreciates, you will face potential losses.

It's essential to conduct thorough research and consider the liquidity, management, and valuation methods associated with these alternative assets before investing. This can be challenging in areas that are not regulated and where mandatory disclosures aren't required. In those situations, the possibility of abuse is significantly elevated.

If you choose to invest in alternatives, through fractional ownership or otherwise, limit your investment to a small portion of your overall portfolio.

Most millennial investors shouldn't bother with alternatives.

Wealthier Tip

Most investors can achieve their financial goals without investing in alternatives.

Chapter 6
Lotto Luck

Everyone dreams of that big win—the big check, the balloons, the financial security, but that's a pipe dream.
—Larry Swedroe, "Avoid the Investment Lottery," *Yahoo Finance*

I have a confession to make.

When the lottery approaches $1 billion, I buy a ticket. I know the odds (about one in 300 million), but I do it anyway. I have all kinds of rationalizations for my behavior like, "Somebody's going to win, why not me?"

I even contemplate what I would do if I won. What team would I have to assemble? How could I use my winnings to make the most significant impact?

I have succumbed to the appeal of lottery-like returns.

Lottery-like Returns in Investing

Becoming an overnight millionaire holds a magnetic appeal. It draws us to risky investments like "penny" stocks, stocks of companies in bankruptcy, IPOs (initial public offerings of companies), and trying to pick the next Amazon or Facebook.

All of these investments share the characteristic of the traditional lottery: The odds of success are very low, but the appeal is the "big hit," if we are lucky.

Understanding how our brain encourages us to gamble instead of investing wisely can help us resist this temptation and get us back on course.

The Role Our Brains Play

Our brains are wired to seek rewards, an evolutionary trait that helped our ancestors survive. Dopamine plays a significant role in our decision-making process.

When we anticipate a monetary gain, the reward system in our brain is activated by releasing both dopamine and testosterone, which provide feelings of gratification.

There's evidence that stock traders who earn profits in several consecutive trades experience the same "high" they would receive from an illegal drug. Their "winning" becomes addictive, pushing them to engage in more risky behavior.

The impact of dopamine on investing decisions has gone mainstream, resulting in terminology like "the dopamine portfolio," which is focused on instant gratification and is built on the fear of missing out.

If you want to fight against the temptation of lottery-like returns, understanding the role of emotions and dopamine release is an excellent first step.

Loss Aversion

"Loss aversion" refers to our tendency to prefer avoiding losses over acquiring equivalent gains. The negative emotional impact of a loss is roughly twice as strong as the positive emotional impact of an equal gain.

When you experience a loss in your investments, you may be more inclined to pursue lottery-like returns, like investing in high-risk stocks or participating in gambling activities, because you don't want to confront your losses.

Wealthier Tip

Once you understand cognitive biases, you can resist the temptation to pursue lottery-like returns.

Chapter 7
Cryptocurrency Confusion

> *Something like Bitcoin, it is a gambling token and it doesn't have any intrinsic value, but that doesn't stop people from wanting to play the roulette wheel.*
> —Warren Buffett, "Bitcoin Price Surges Above $30,500; but Warren Buffett Still Thinks it's a Gamble," *Investor's Business Daily*

If you want to invest a small part of your discretionary funds in cryptocurrency, that's a personal decision.

No one really knows whether cryptocurrency market prices will tank or explode, so making a significant investment in cryptocurrency may keep you from reaching your goals.

What is Cryptocurrency?

Cryptocurrency is a virtual currency that uses cryptography for security. It can be used as an alternative payment method or as an investment.

Cryptocurrencies are tracked by "blockchain," which records transactions. They are commonly created through "mining," a process involving computers solving complex problems to verify the authenticity of transactions.

You can purchase cryptocurrency from an exchange or another user.

There are more than 22,000 different cryptocurrencies traded publicly. The best-known one is Bitcoin (BTRC-USD). Others include Ethereum (ETH-USD) and Litecoin (LTC-USD).

Cryptocurrency Pros

Proponents of investing in cryptocurrencies find it appealing that government entities have no control over the value of cryptocurrencies and believe they are safe and secure.

Some also believe having cryptocurrencies adds to the diversification of your portfolio because the value of cryptocurrencies doesn't correlate with the price of stocks and bonds.

They believe Bitcoin, in particular, can act as a hedge against inflation because there's a limit on the number of coins issued. The maximum number of Bitcoins that can be issued is 21 million. It's projected to reach that limit in 2140.

For some investors, the anonymity of investing in cryptocurrency is a plus. You don't have to provide identification or submit a background or credit check.

Cryptocurrency Cons

The security of cryptocurrencies is not absolute since there is the possibility of an attack on a blockchain, which could cause havoc.

The safety of cryptocurrency investments is disputed. Bank deposits are insured by the U.S. government. Your online cryptocurrency "wallet" is not.

The anonymous nature of cryptocurrency transactions is misleading. Cryptocurrency transactions leave a digital trail that federal agencies can potentially decode.

There are also troublesome issues relating to the need for uniform regulation of cryptocurrencies, which add uncertainty to these transactions. While cryptocurrency is currently legal in the U.S., China does not recognize cryptocurrencies as legal tender and prohibits their circulation.

Recently, there have been issues with cryptocurrency platforms. A leading exchange, FTX, filed for bankruptcy protection in November 2022. Its former CEO, Sam Bankman-Fried, has been convicted of seven counts of wire fraud and conspiracy.

The SEC has sued Binance, the world's largest cryptocurrency exchange, accusing it of artificially inflating trading volumes and failing to control U.S. accounts. The chief executive of Binance, Changpeng Zhao, pleaded guilty to failing to maintain an effective money laundering program. The company agreed to pay a penalty of $4 billion to end multiple federal investigations.

There are no legal protections when you make a cryptocurrency payment, unlike your ability to dispute charges when you use a credit or debit card.

Cryptocurrency mining also has a significant adverse impact on the environment. According to EarthJustice, Cryptocurrency mining exploded in the U.S. after it was banned in China in 2021.

Bitcoin consumed an estimated 36 billion kilowatt hours of electricity from July 2021 to July 2022. This massive consumption increases carbon emissions and worsens air quality.

Cryptocurrency mining released more than 27.4 million tons of carbon dioxide into the environment between mid-2021 and 2022. According to Climate.gov by adding more carbon dioxide to the atmosphere, the natural greenhouse effect is supercharged, which causes global temperatures to rise.

Don't Speculate

If you wouldn't consider putting a large portion of your retirement funds in a highly speculative stock, you shouldn't do the same with cryptocurrency.

According to Schwab, "Bitcoin and other cryptocurrencies are highly speculative investments since supply and demand drive their volatility—not intrinsic value."

Wealthier Tip

Don't let investing in cryptocurrency distract you from reaching your financial goals.

Chapter 8
Investing Myths

The overwhelmingly large number of investors should seek membership in the passive management club. This group, instead of scratching for a small edge in today's extraordinarily efficient markets, wisely accepts what the markets deliver.
—Charles D. Ellis, *Winning the Loser's Game: Timeless Strategies for Successful Investing*

The key to success in investing is sound wisdom, but it can be hard to come by in today's media crowded with voices who claim they know what's best for you. The key is knowing who to ignore.

Here are some of the biggest investment myths and the evidence that debunks them.

Myth: Trading on margin is a good idea.

Trading on margin involves borrowing money to invest in stocks, effectively leveraging your investments. The idea is that you can amplify your gains. However, this myth is fraught with risks that can lead to substantial losses.

Truth: Trading on margin is risky.

Margin trading magnifies both gains and losses. When markets are volatile, as they often are, it's easy to get caught in a downward spiral of debt. History has shown that excessive margin trading contributed to market crashes, like the Great Depression in the 1930s and the Dot-com bubble in the early 2000s.

Investing on margin also requires you to pay interest, which negatively impacts your returns.

Myth: Day trading is a good idea.

Day trading, where investors buy and sell assets within the same trading day, has gained popularity thanks to the allure of quick profits. However, it's a myth that day trading is a sustainable and profitable long-term strategy.

Truth: Day trading yields loss.

Research shows that the vast majority of day traders incur significant losses over time. One study found that over 80% of day traders lose money, with less than 1% consistently making profits.

Myth: Investing in gold makes sense.

Gold has been considered a safe-haven asset for centuries. Many investors believe it's a reliable hedge against economic turmoil. However, the notion that investing in gold is always a sound strategy is a myth.

Truth: Gold has underperformed U.S. stocks.

While gold can serve as a safe-haven asset and a hedge against inflation, its long-term returns are not as impressive as many believe. From 1971 to 2022, U.S. stocks had an average annual return of 10.21%, compared to 7.78% for gold.

A more compelling argument against investing in gold is that it's only worth what someone else is willing to pay for it when you want to sell. Unlike investing in companies with the potential to make a profit, gold doesn't generate income.

The historical performance of gold isn't indicative of future prices.

Myth: Stock picking and market timing make sense.

Many investors believe they can outsmart the market by picking individual stocks and timing their buys and sells to maximize profits. However, this myth ignores evidence that suggests otherwise.

Truth: Passive strategies earn more.

Research consistently shows that actively managed portfolios, where fund managers attempt to pick winning stocks and time the market, underperform passive, index-based strategies over the long term. In fact, the majority of professional fund managers fail to consistently beat their benchmark indices.

Myth: Technical trading makes sense.

Technical analysis involves analyzing past price movements and patterns to predict future stock prices. It's a myth that this approach is a reliable way to make investment decisions.

Truth: Technical analysis isn't effective.

Numerous studies have shown that technical analysis is no more effective than random chance when it comes to predicting stock price movements. Technical traders often rely on subjective interpretations of charts, which can lead to inconsistent and inaccurate predictions.

Myth: Always invest in stocks of high-quality companies.

Stocks of high-quality companies, characterized by stability and strong fundamentals, offer higher expected returns compared to riskier stocks.

Truth: Sometimes riskier is better.

Stocks of high-quality companies are perceived as less risky and offer lower expected returns. While they provide stability and lower volatility, more volatile stocks have the potential for higher returns.

Focusing on high-quality company stocks has another downside. One study found that only four percent of listed companies explain the net gain for the entire U.S. stock market since 1926. The returns of the other stocks collectively matched Treasury Bills.

If you limit your investments to high-quality stocks (or stocks with other characteristics), it's likely you will miss the tiny percentage of outperforming stocks.

To build a robust investment strategy, consider the investing strategies discussed in Chapters 1 and 2. By following these evidence-based principles, you can increase your chances of achieving your financial goals.

Myth: Spend time researching individual stocks.

Many investors believe thorough research before buying stocks is beneficial and necessary for successful investing.

Truth: Research is a waste of time.

Stock prices are influenced by various factors, including unpredictable future events. Your research is unlikely to uncover anything that isn't already in the public domain and known to millions of other investors. Those investors buy and sell stocks every minute of every day.

How likely is it that the price the market sets on a stock is too low or too high?

If you are buying or selling a stock, there's someone on the other side of the trade whose evaluation is different from yours. How confident are you that you are "right" and they are "wrong?"

Myth: Why settle for average returns?

Don't be misled when you're told that index-based returns are "average" or that investing in index funds and ETFs is "fine for beginners."

Truth: The returns of the index aren't "average."

For the 15 years ended June 30, 2023, according to the SPIVA reports, 95.80% of all U.S. large-cap core funds *underperformed* the S&P 500 index.

If you owned a low-fee index fund that tracked the same index, your returns (which would be reduced by low management fees) would have been superior to the returns of most actively managed funds that attempted to beat that index.

That's not "average".

Myth: You can get higher returns with lower risk.

It's easy to be tempted by investments that promise high returns with little risk. Most often, the returns are illusory and the risk is far greater than what is disclosed.

Truth: Many investments are too good to be true.

With minor exceptions, an investment strategy that pays more interest than Treasury Bills or Notes (or promises a higher return) for a comparable period is either a fraud or involves more risk than buying Treasuries.

Myth: Invest in past "winners."

Mutual funds with a good recent track record tout their historical performance. The implication is that past performance is predictive of the future.

It isn't.

Truth: The past doesn't predict the future.

Past performance doesn't predict future results. Investment decisions should be based on more than just historical returns.

James Choi, a Professor of Finance at Yale, studied the relationship between past returns and future returns and found, "If anything, over the past two decades, you seem to do a little bit worse if you chase past returns on mutual funds."

Myth: Reliable advice is found in popular finance books.

If you read something in a book about investing, it's easy to believe it must be accurate.

That's not always the case.

Truth: Popular advice isn't usually wise.

There are many books touting market timing strategies, stock picking systems, and books about "technical analysis." There's little credible academic support for any of these investing practices.

For example, in *The 9 Steps to Financial Freedom,* Suze Orman states that owning one mutual fund provides a diversified portfolio "because you own a little of everything they're invested in."

Many mutual funds are narrowly focused on a particular industry or market like energy, real estate, or healthcare. Owning one of these funds *doesn't* provide a properly diversified portfolio and may expose you to unsuitable risk.

Radio host Dave Ramsey, in his book, *The Total Money Makeover*, believes a safe withdrawal rate for your retirement money is 8%.

Fidelity Investments is more accurate: "For a high degree of confidence that you can cover a consistent amount of expenses in retirement (i.e., it should work 90% of the time), aim to withdraw no more than 4% to 5% of your savings in the first year of retirement, and then adjust the amount every year for inflation."

James Choi, the Yale professor referenced earlier in this Chapter, reviewed 50 of the most-popular finance books and found they frequently deviated from sound, academically based advice. He concluded that popular advice is sometimes driven by "fallacies."

Why Are There So Many Myths About Investing?

- **Human psychology:** Investing often involves complex decisions and uncertainty, which can create anxiety and fear. We're naturally drawn to stories and myths that promise easy and quick solutions, even if those solutions are unrealistic.
- **Overconfidence bias:** Many investors tend to overestimate their own abilities and believe that they can beat the market or make better investment decisions than others. This overconfidence can lead to the propagation of investment myths.
- **Confirmation bias:** People often seek information that confirms their existing beliefs and biases. If someone believes in a particular investment myth, they are more likely to share information that supports that belief, creating a self-reinforcing cycle.
- **Financial industry interests:** The financial industry may have an interest in promoting certain investment products or strategies, even if they are not in the best interest of individual investors. This can lead to the dissemination of misleading information.
- **Lack of financial education:** Many individuals lack a solid understanding of financial principles and investment strategies. This knowledge gap makes them vulnerable to investment myths and misinformation.

- **Media sensationalism:** The media often highlights stories of extraordinary success or failure in investing. These sensational stories can lead to unrealistic expectations and misconceptions about how investing works.
- **Herd mentality:** Investors sometimes follow the crowd and adopt popular investment trends or myths. This herd mentality perpetuates myths.
- **Fear of missing out:** The fear of missing out on potential gains can drive investors to make impulsive decisions based on rumors and unreliable information.

Wealthier Tip

Shun investing myths that impede your ability to implement a simple and easy investment strategy grounded in peer-reviewed research.

Chapter 9
Terrible Consequences

According to our results, movements in stock markets have a clear and recognizable effect on percentage change in suicide rates across 36 countries.
—Tomasz Piotr Wisniewski; Brendan John Lambe; Keshab Shrestha, *Do Stock Market Fluctuations Affect Suicide Rates?* (July 13, 2018)

Have you ever considered your relationship with investing? It may feel like a battlefield scarred by losses and disappointments rather than an enriching experience.

You're far from alone in this sentiment. Many find their association with investing mirroring the strains of a toxic relationship, sapping their mental energy and emotional resilience.

Much of the blame should be placed squarely on the financial media.

A Source of Misinformation

The financial press emphasizes fear, uncertainty, and drama to attract attention, which generates anxiety and may cause you to make impulsive investment decisions.

It pushes simplistic narratives that a single factor causes every market event, which overlooks the complexity of financial markets and sets unrealistic expectations.

It encourages investors to chase fleeting trends and opinions and amplifies hype and rumors that spread misinformation and distort asset prices in the short run. Here's sound advice about the financial media from *Retirement Researcher*: "The first thing to do is to stop paying attention to the financial media. This is easier said than done, but it's important. Even when you understand what they're doing, the financial media is good at getting you firmly aboard the fear vs. greed roller coaster (it *is* their job, after all.)."

Tragic Consequences

It's not difficult to find gut-wrenching stories of investors who relied on misinformation and got hurt badly.

Alex Kearns was a 20-year-old trader who used a popular trading app, Robinhood. Kearns thought he had racked up hundreds of thousands in losses, but he misread his statement and believed his losses were higher than they actually were.

In his suicide note, he accused Robinhood of permitting him to take on too much risk and complained that he was given an inappropriate amount of credit, which permitted him to trade excessively.

The day after he took his own life, Robinhood sent him an automated e-mail indicating the trade in question was resolved and he didn't owe any money.

Sadly, this is not an isolated tragedy.

One comprehensive study used a sample of data from 36 countries (including the U.S.) and found a significant increase in suicide rates correlated with a decrease in stock market returns. The authors of the study recommended "proactive suicide prevention strategies" for those who could be affected by the vagaries of the stock market.

It may not be an exaggeration to state your life may depend on following peer-reviewed, academically based investment advice. While bad financial decisions may not end your life, they'll certainly hinder your goals and wreak havoc on your quality of life.

Wealthier Tip

Don't underestimate the consequences of relying on misinformation disseminated by the financial media.

74

Part Three
The Ugly Reality

It's bad.

Chapter 10
Something Needs to Change

Only 48 percent of U.S. adults say they have enough emergency savings to cover at least three months' worth of expenses.
—Lane Gillespie, "Bankrate's 2023 Annual Emergency Savings Report," *Bankrate*

The financial state of a shocking number of Americans is chilling.

Many, including high earners, are spending beyond their means and living paycheck to paycheck. They're saddled with debt and lack sufficient savings for emergencies, let alone retirement. While the American dream promises prosperity and upward mobility, the financial reality for many is far from this ideal.

Here are just a few factors that illustrate the desperate financial situation many people face.

Insufficient Savings

An integral component of retirement readiness is personal savings. Yet, according to an Employee Benefit Research Institute survey, only 68% of American workers reported having *any* retirement savings in 2022. A stunning 34% said that the total value of their savings and investments, excluding the value of their primary home, was less than $25,000.

Compounding the problem, a Bankrate survey found that a quarter of Americans couldn't muster $1,000 for an emergency expense without resorting to a credit card and paying it off incrementally.

Millennials find saving particularly challenging. They have other priorities like paying off debt, building emergency savings, raising children, and supporting their parents.

Student loan debt is a primary culprit. One study found that 40% of millennial households between the ages of 28 and 38 had student loan debt that amounted to more than 40% of their income.

It's not surprising that millennials are behind older investors when it comes to retirement savings.

Overreliance on Social Security

According to the Social Security Administration, 37% of older men and 42% of older women receiving Social Security benefits rely on it for at least 50% of their income, and 12% of men and 15% of women depend on Social Security for 90% or more of their income.

Considering that the average monthly Social Security benefit for retired workers and dependents is a meager $1,788, it's easy to imagine their financial difficulties.

Escalating Healthcare Costs

The Fidelity Retiree Health Care Cost Estimate suggests that an average retired couple aged 65 in 2022 might need approximately $315,000 (after tax) to cover healthcare expenses during retirement.

There's no way people who rely primarily on Social Security can afford these costs.

Consumer Debt

According to The Federal Reserve Bank of New York's Center for Microeconomic Data, household debt in the second quarter of 2023 increased to $17.06 trillion. Credit card balances increased to $1.03 trillion.

Other components of household debt include mortgage debt, a home equity line of credit, student debt, and auto debt.

No wonder so many Americans don't have an emergency fund. They're struggling to pay off their consumer debt.

In a recent survey, 37% of those 55 to 64 reported difficulty meeting their financial obligations. Almost 30% of those 65 years and older are "struggling to pay their expenses."

Millennials are racking up consumer debt at an alarming pace. Those ages 30 to 38 hold nearly $4 trillion of total household debt, a significant increase over prior years.

Now is the time to change, especially if you're young.

Wealthier Tip

Take a hard look at your financial situation and start making necessary changes.

Chapter II

A
Rigged System

Representatives and lobbyists of the financial sector are so entwined with the agencies that are supposed to regulate it that Washingtonians collectively refer to them as "The Blob."
—Gautam Mukunda, "The Price of Wall Street's Power," *Harvard Business Review*

As a DIY investor, you're engaged with a system rigged against your interests. Your first step toward financial empowerment is understanding how the securities industry and the financial media work together to keep you from reaching your goals.

Big Vested Interests

The securities industry is huge in size and profits. As of 2022, there were 620,882 registered representatives in the U.S. employed by 3,378 securities firms.

In 2021, broker-dealers generated gross revenues totaling $398.6 billion, yielding a pre-tax net income of $91.8 billion, translating into a profit margin of a whopping 23.06%.

The securities industry also deploys hundreds of lobbyists. Open Secrets (a research group tracking money in U.S. politics and its effect on elections and public policy) said the industry spent over $139 million in 2022 to sway political decision-making.

That money is mainly spent to keep your cash flowing into their pockets.

Lobbying that Harms Investors

Here's how those lobbying efforts harm investors.

The financial services industry is unique. It regulates itself "through little-discussed, structurally-entrenched self-regulatory organizations," of which FINRA (the Financial Industry Regulatory Authority) is the most prominent. FINRA is charged with ensuring the integrity of America's financial system, working under the supposed supervision of the Securities and Exchange Commission.

There's legitimate concern that FINRA advances the interest of the securities industry over those of investors, "limiting [investors'] ability to save for the future."

Benjamin P. Edwards, an Associate Professor of Law at the University of Nevada School of Law, observed that "FINRA's structure poses a continual risk that industry members will subvert its processes to act like a cartel, promoting industry interests at the expense of the public and contributing to the excessive rents collected by financial intermediaries."

His analysis found that the "public" representatives serving on FINRA's Board of Governors "...often simultaneously serve on the boards of corporate financial intermediaries, giving rise to conflicts of interest between loyalties to market participants and industry lobbying groups and their roles as protectors of the public interest."

The securities industry has successfully lobbied for less stringent obligations of brokers to their clients.

No Jury Trial for You

The most pernicious impact of self-regulation is the imposition of mandatory arbitration. Most investors are unaware that as a condition of opening a brokerage account, they must give up their constitutional right to a jury trial and agree to submit all disputes to the FINRA-run arbitration system.

Efforts to abolish this requirement have been unavailing.

As William D. Cohan noted in an article in *The New York Times*, "...not only is forced arbitration a major curbing of legal rights, but FINRA's version of arbitration also comes with an additional dollop of what seems like bias."

The bias includes an informational advantage brokerage firms have as "repeat players" to select arbitrators more inclined to rule in their favor.

Another troubling issue about FINRA arbitration is the lack of diversity of its arbitrators. Its own statistics indicate that 65% of its arbitrators are male, 76% are white, only 5% have LGBTQ status, and 42% are 70 or older.

FINRA arbitrators don't have to provide reasons for their decisions. While an appeal is technically possible, overturning arbitration awards is challenging.

It's not surprising that almost every consumer group supports abolishing mandatory arbitration, yet it persists, thanks to effective lobbying.

A Failed System

Given the vast resources devoted to "helping" investors achieve retirement goals, it's appropriate to ask: How is this system working for you?

Not well?

Here's why:

Poor investment results: The "behavior gap"—the difference between the returns generated by investments (like mutual funds) and the returns that investors realize—is a pressing concern.

Morningstar reported that over the decade ending December 31, 2021, investors earned about 9.3% per year on the average dollar invested in mutual and exchange-traded funds (ETFs). However, these returns were 1.7% *lower* than the actual returns earned by these investments over that period.

What causes this "gap?"

Investors bounce in and out of these funds, often at inopportune times. According to *Morningstar*, this behavior costs investors "nearly one-sixth the return they would have earned if they had simply bought and held."

A wealth of misinformation: What are the root causes of the sad state of financial readiness for so many Americans?

Their information source is often the financial media, as discussed in Chapter 9. Commission-based brokers add to the problem. Unethical brokers may be financially incentivized to engage in excessive trading to generate commissions or to recommend investment products that generate the highest commission.

Why Participate?

You might ask: "Why should I invest in a system rigged against me?"

Here's why.

- **Historical performance:** Over the long term, the stock market has historically outperformed many other investment vehicles. According to data from the S&P 500 index (one of the primary indices used to gauge the performance of the U.S. stock market), the average annual return from 1928 to 2022 was 9.81% (assuming you reinvested all dividends).
- **Inflation protection:** Americans are understandably concerned about inflation. The rise in prices over time reduces the purchasing power of your money. By investing in stocks, which historically offer higher returns than inflation, your money has the potential to grow and keep pace with rising prices.

Although you pay a price for this protection (because stocks are volatile and subject to losing value over the short term), you will reap the benefit of capturing stock market returns over the long term.

- **Compound growth:** The power of compound growth means your investments earn returns, and then those returns earn returns, leading to meaningful growth over time.
- **Diversification:** The stock market offers an opportunity to spread risk across sectors and individual companies. Rather than putting all your money into one company or industry, you can diversify your portfolio and mitigate losses you might incur from investing in one company or industry.
- **Liquidity:** One of the significant benefits of stock market investments is liquidity. Stocks and mutual funds can be bought or sold on stock exchanges, offering easy access to your money when needed compared to less liquid investments like real estate and private equity.

Even with these benefits, you need to work the system to your advantage.

Wealthier Tip

Realize the system is stacked against you. You desperately need accurate, objective information. Now you have it.

Part Four
Practice Stoic Finance

The right mindset.

Chapter 12
Letting Go

We cannot choose our external circumstances, but we can always choose how we respond to them.
—Epictetus, A Greek philosopher of 1st and early 2nd centuries C.E., and an exponent of Stoic ethics

As an investor, you're bombarded with the next "big thing" in investing, from cryptocurrency to hot stock tips that promise the moon. But what determines your investing success is founded in a philosophy over two millennia old: Stoicism.

How can an ancient philosophy make a tangible difference in modern investment strategies for the digital generation?

What is Stoicism?

At its inception, Stoicism was a guide for living a life of virtue and wisdom. It distinguishes between what we can control, our actions, thoughts, and feelings, and what we cannot—everything else.

A core principle of Stoicism is accepting your fate by understanding the limits of your control.

Stoics focus their energy on striving for personal excellence by practicing four cardinal virtues: wisdom, courage, justice, and temperance. It embraces a framework for leading a virtuous life by cultivating inner strength, wisdom, and emotional resilience.

Embrace the Stoic Investor Mindset

Investing is as much about managing emotions and expectations as it is about managing money. The Stoic principles of focusing on what is within our control and accepting what is not are especially critical in investing.

- **Accept market volatility.** The stock markets are inherently volatile, unpredictable, and influenced by factors beyond your control. Once you accept this fact, you can manage your money calmly without being influenced by the stock market's daily gyrations.
- **Ignore the noise.** The constant barrage of stock predictions, market gossip, and economic forecasts can be overwhelming. A stoic mindset filters out this noise and recognizes that much is beyond our control and irrelevant to our long-term investment strategy.
- **Control what you can.** Applying Stoicism to investing isn't about disengagement but proactive focus. It's a strategy that reduces the volume of external noise to amplify personal financial intuition and wisdom. Stoic investing is not a passive resignation to fate but an active cultivation of an unshakeable core from which all investment decisions emanate.

By letting go of the factors you can't control—like market movements and interest rates—and focusing on what you can, you harness a stoic edge, which promotes a healthier relationship with investing, defined by personal values, discipline, and an even-keeled disposition.

Here are some facts that are within your control:

- **Your investment strategy:** Your investment approach should be personal—tailored to your goals, risk tolerance, and time horizon.
- **Your savings:** Regular investment contributions smooth out investment costs over time and build your nest egg.
- **Your emotions:** Stoicism doesn't demand a total lack of emotion. Instead, it encourages emotional intelligence to "stand back, breathe and survey the emotional landscape." Keeping a cool head when the market is in chaos allows for decision-making based on reason, not fear, anxiety, or greed.
- **Your financial education:** You have the power to educate yourself about investments, the markets, and financial planning. As an informed investor, you'll be better positioned to make decisions that align with your investment philosophy.
- **Your time horizon:** A Stoic investor views time as a companion. The

ancient Roman Stoic philosopher Lucius Annaeus Seneca had this sage view of the value of time: "People are frugal guarding their personal property, but as soon as it comes to squandering time, they are most wasteful of the one thing in which it is right to be stingy."

The longer your investment horizon, the better you can absorb the shocks of short-term market movements and align with the historical upward trend of markets.

Stoic Exercises for the Mindful Investor

Here are some exercises that will reinforce a stoic mindset and improve your investment outcome:

- **Practice dispassion.** Analyze investment opportunities focusing on data and fundamentals, not hype or emotion.
- **Focus on the present.** Act based on the present circumstances, not out of regret for past losses or fear of future downturns.
- **Prepare for adversity.** Financially and mentally prepare for market downturns. Understand they are part of investing.
- **Contemplate legacy.** Consider what financial legacy you want to create. Reflect on the long-term impact of your investments.
- **Be mindful.** Mindfulness in investing leads to a more disciplined, serene, and ultimately successful financial life. The Stoic investor's path is about building wealth and fostering a life of virtue and purpose through investing.

Wealthier Tip

Integrate the principles of Stoicism into your investing to build the right mindset for financial success.

Chapter 13
Perspective Power

Although it may be tempting to sell down your investments to cash to avoid seeing a drop in the value of your assets, having perspective will encourage you to stay invested and remain disciplined to your investment strategy.
—EPG Wealth, "What is the Power of Perspective when Investing?"

Here's wisdom from legendary investor Warren Buffett: "If you aren't willing to own a stock for ten years, don't even think about owning it for 10 minutes."

Buffett has perspective.

In 2022, when the S&P 500 index lost 18% of its value, I was contacted by a distraught investor. He was upset that the value of his 401(k) plan had declined.

I asked him how old he was. He was 38. I asked if he had plans to access his money early. He didn't (he can't withdraw from his 401(k) plan without penalty, with some exceptions, until age 59½).

Why was he concerned about the value of his 401(k) plan 21 years before he would access it? He didn't have perspective.

Having perspective empowers you to incorporate a stoic mindset into your investment decisions.

Money is Emotional

Perspective requires dispassionately looking at data and making rational decisions based on logic. However, the subject of money is intensely emotional.

More than 74% of those responding to an online survey of members of the Financial Planning Association reported that during a planning session, a client became emotionally distraught (started crying, trembling, sobbing, or becoming violent).

Why is the subject of money so fraught with emotion?

- The fear of not having enough money to sustain ourselves or our loved ones creates anxiety, stress, and fear.
- Limited financial resources or debt makes us feel trapped or dependent on others, leading to frustration, vulnerability, or resentment.
- Money is often associated with social status and success. It can influence our self-worth and how we perceive ourselves compared to others. Financial struggles or the perception of falling behind others can lead to feelings of inferiority, envy, or shame.
- Money can be tied to emotional experiences, like inheritance, windfalls, or losses. Positive or adverse money-related events can trigger joy, excitement, grief, or disappointment. Our past experiences and beliefs around money shape our emotional reactions to financial situations.
- Money can impact our relationships with family, friends, or romantic partners. Disagreements about spending, debt, or differing financial values can lead to conflict and tension. Financial dependency or disputes over money can strain relationships and evoke strong emotions like resentment, jealousy, or guilt.
- The belief that money is hard to come by can create a scarcity mindset. This mindset can lead to fear, anxiety, or a constant drive to accumulate more money. The fear of scarcity can intensify emotional responses related to money.

Understanding the Brain and Emotions

Imagine your brain being flooded with all these emotions and then being asked to remain calm, relaxed, and objective. Emotions are likely to prevail over acting rationally.

If you understand how the brain processes emotionally charged subjects, you'll be better equipped to manage money during stressful times.

Studies in neuroscience have found that emotions originate from the amygdala, a brain region responsible for emotional processing. In highly charged emotional states, the amygdala can overwhelm the prefrontal cortex, the brain's rational decision-making center. This process, known as "amygdala hijack" can lead to irrational behavior.

The emotionally overwhelmed brain has great difficulty processing and acting on rational information. Here's how to overcome amygdala hijack:

- **Recognize the signs.** Learn to identify the early symptoms of an amygdala hijack, like increased heart rate, rapid breathing, or a surge of intense emotions. Awareness of these signs can help you intervene before the hijack takes complete control.
- **Pause and breathe.** When you notice the signs of an amygdala hijack, pause and focus on your breath. Deep, slow breaths activate the body's relaxation response and help calm the amygdala, allowing you to regain control over your emotions.
- **Name your emotions.** Psychiatrist Dr. David Siegel is credited with identifying a technique called "Name it to tame it." He found that simply "naming" emotions alleviates the stress those emotions cause. When you feel an emotion, say what it is—anger, fear, excitement—to calm your brain.
- **Engage logical thinking.** The amygdala hijack overrides rational thought, so it's essential to engage your analytical mind consciously. Remind yourself of the facts and consider the situation more objectively. This conscious activity can help counterbalance your emotional response and permit you to make better decisions.
- **Take a break.** Remove yourself from the triggering situation temporarily. Stepping away and engaging in a different activity can help create distance and allow your emotions to settle. Take a walk, meditate, or engage in a calming hobby to regain composure.
- **Develop emotional intelligence.** Strengthening your emotional intelligence can help manage amygdala hijack. Improve self-awareness, understand your triggers, and develop strategies to regulate emotions effectively. Techniques like mindfulness, journaling, and therapy can support this process.
- **Practice stress management.** Chronic stress can increase the likelihood

of amygdala hijack. Taking care of your overall well-being can help minimize its impact.

Overcoming amygdala hijack takes practice and patience. It's an ongoing process of self-awareness and emotional regulation.

Bulls and Bears

Now you're ready to review data and process it rationally.

The stock market is volatile by nature. When the stock market swings up or down, intense emotions are triggered.

A stock index is considered a bear market when the closing price drops at least 20% from its most recent high. A bull market starts when the closing price has risen 20% from its recent low.

In a bear market, stocks lose 35% on average, which is unsettling. In a bull market, stocks gain 114% on average. This is exciting.

Now for some perspective:

- Since 1928, there have been 27 bear markets and the same number of bull markets in the S&P 500 index.
- Bear markets last an average of 292 days (9.7 months).
- Bull markets have an average length of 992 days (2.7 years).

Wait It Out

When your portfolio of stocks is down significantly, it's unsurprising that you may listen to the pundits and "flee to safety." But what would happen if you resisted this temptation and did nothing?

Look at these returns for the S&P 500 index from 2000–2007:

2000	-9.03	2004	10.74
2001	-11.85	2005	4.83
2002	-21.97	2006	15.61
2003	28.36	2007	5.48

During the three years of negative returns from 2000-2002, many investors were no doubt tempted to give up and reduce or even eliminate their exposure to stocks.

If they did nothing, they were rewarded with five consecutive years of positive returns and generated an overall return from 2003-2007 of over 13%.

There's no assurance the future will replicate past recoveries, but over the long term, the stock market has increased in value.

Over the short term, it's a bumpy ride.

Being patient is the secret to long-term investing success.

Wealthier Tip

Historical perspective helps you implement a stoic mindset with your investing.

Chapter 14
Don't Look

Looking at your portfolio frequently can make you feel like it's performing worse than it actually is, and the less likely you'll invest correctly for long-term success.
—Dan Egan, "Nearly Half of Investors Check Their Performance at Least Once a Day—Here's Why That's a Problem," *CNBC*

I'm a long-term investor. I don't care about short-term market volatility. I know how upset I would feel if I checked my portfolio value during a down market and saw the amount of my unrealized losses. I have two rules about when to check my portfolio:

I do so as infrequently as possible—no more than once or twice a year.
When I'm tempted, I only check when the market is up.

There are sound, evidence-based reasons why you should follow my example.

A Stoic Twist

Stoic philosopher Marcus Aurelius, quoting the Greek Philosopher Democritus, said: "Do little if you want contentment of mind."

Aurelius added a stoic twist that we should do only what is necessary for achieving our goals. He regarded, "the majority of our words and actions" as "anything but necessary" and urged us to dispense with them.

His timeless advice has particular applicability to investing.

Why Do We Want to Look?

As long-term investors, we understand that short-term market volatility is just normal noise that should be ignored. Obsessively reacting to the news only creates stress and anxiety.

Then why do we do it?

A combination of cognitive biases and the neuroscience of reward can explain our behavior. Understanding these motivations can help overcome bad habits.

The endowment effect: This bias refers to how when we hold investments, we value them more than if others held them.

If I told you I owned VT, and you didn't, it's unlikely you would check the value of VT. But if you own it, you place a high value on it. You feel a need to keep track of it.

Loss aversion: It's painful to experience losses—even paper ones. We feel compelled to check to see how much our portfolio has declined.

Information bias: This is the tendency to seek and evaluate information even if it's irrelevant. We believe more information is valuable, even though less would be far more helpful in keeping us on track.

We ignore the fact that investing intelligently and responsibly requires minimal effort. Acting on the information generated by the financial media (like daily highs and lows, analyst reports, and "breaking news") harms your investment returns.

Brain chemistry: When our portfolio increases in value, our brain releases dopamine. Each time we check our investments and find they've grown in value, that "reward" reinforces this behavior.

There's a flip side. When our portfolio decreases in value, the hypothalamus in the brain releases a hormone that starts a process resulting in the release of cortisol, a steroid hormone, into our bloodstream. Too much cortisol can have adverse health consequences.

Don't look. It's far easier to remain calm when you aren't obsessively checking your portfolio. It's simple to reduce stress, lower anxiety, and reap the benefit of the stock market, which has a long history of increasing in value over the long term.

Here is an additional benefit. According to Marcus Aurelius, dispensing with unnecessary activity will give you "greater leisure and a less troubled mind."

Wealthier Tip

Inattention to your portfolio is a virtue that will pay financial and emotional dividends.

Chapter 15
Masterly Inactivity

Inactivity strikes us as intelligent behavior.
—Warren Buffett, "Berkshire Hathaway Letters to Shareholders, 1965-2018 by Warren Buffet," Max Leonard Almeda, *Medium*

Just because you believe it's necessary to look at your portfolio, that doesn't mean you should make any changes, particularly when those decisions are likely to be influenced by emotions like fear.

As indicated in Chapter 12, Stoics believe a critical component of managing fear is recognizing factors outside our control. Stoics don't spend time focusing on those factors. Instead, they focus on what's within their control, like "thoughts, beliefs and actions."

You can't control a decline in the value of your investments, but you can control how you deal with it.

Your strategy should be to stay the course and resist the temptation to bounce in and out of the stock market. As stated by Vanguard founder John Bogle, "Don't do something, stand there."

If you invested in the S&P 500 index fund and missed the 10 best days in the market from 1993-2011, your returns would have been diminished by 54% over being invested during that entire period.

You can understand why attempting to time the market by bouncing in and out is dumb.

Good year? Bad year?

2022 was a bad year for both the stock and bond markets—a perfect storm for investors who relied on the bond portion of their portfolio to mitigate losses when stocks tanked.

VT, the all-world stock ETF recommended in Chapter 1, lost 18.45% of its value.

SHY, the bond ETF, lost 3.88% of its value.

Suppose your portfolio was in a 60% (VT) and 40% (SHY) asset allocation. Your portfolio lost 12.62% of its value. That's a big hit. If your portfolio was worth $100,000 at the start of 2022, it ended the year down by $12,622.

Bad year, right?

Not necessarily. It depends on your metric for success.

Realized vs. Unrealized Losses

There's a critical difference between a realized and an unrealized loss.

A realized loss occurs when you lock in a loss by selling an investment for less than you paid. An unrealized loss is just on paper because you still hold the investment.

If you didn't sell the ETFs you held in 2022, you had only unrealized losses. If you sold, you converted them into actual losses.

The Challenge of Doing Nothing

When you don't respond to market volatility by taking action, you don't convert unrealized losses into realized ones. You trust the market to recover your losses over time.

We don't know what will happen, but history tells us the market goes up over the long term (see the discussion on perspective in Chapter 13).

What you do—or better, don't do—in the short term matters.

If our hypothetical investor was asked at the end of 2022 whether it was a good or bad year, the response should be:

> *It was a good year. Although the stock and bond market was down, I didn't convert unrealized losses into realized ones. I engaged in masterly inactivity. I continued to invest and took advantage of lower prices. When the markets recover, I will be well-positioned to recover my losses and start on the path to positive earnings over the long term.*

Suppose you want to emulate the experience of this investor. You'll watch your portfolio decline. You'll be inundated with misinformation by the financial media and the securities industry. They want you to "take action."

Here are some subconscious feelings you may experience pushing you to act contrary to your best interest.

- **Recency bias:** We overreact to recent experiences. When the market tanks, it isn't easy to envision a recovery. Instead, we catastrophize and believe further declines are more likely, even though the opposite may be true.
- **Herding behavior:** We are inclined to follow others and imitate their behavior rather than act objectively and rationally. If we believe others are selling in a down market, we may be influenced to follow suit.
- **Cortisol increase:** When we see the value of our portfolio decline, we feel understandably stressed, as indicated by higher cortisol levels in the body. One study of London traders found that increased stress levels made them more cautious rather than more objective.
- **Confirmation bias:** We favor information that confirms preexisting beliefs. Confirmation bias may cause us to overweight negative information about further market declines instead of objectively considering data about the long-term history of the market. This bias can cause us to "do something" when the prudent course would be to " do nothing."

If you are interested in exploring this area further, I highly recommend *Thinking, Fast and Slow* by Daniel Kahneman. It discusses cognitive biases in depth and explores the two conflicting ways we think about issues: intuitive and deliberate.

Wealthier Tip

Engage in masterly inactivity and embrace the prospect of converting unrealized market losses into future gains.

Chapter 16
Don't Be Intimidated

When you hear some "advanced" strategies, such as rebalancing, tax loss harvesting, or in this case tax efficient asset placement, you should assess how much the strategy really applies to you and how much difference it actually makes.
—Harry Sit, "When Tax Efficient Asset Placement Doesn't Make Much Difference," *The Finance Buff*

Stoics "shun complexity and worship simplicity."

The stoic mindset will embrace the simple investing strategy set forth in Chapter 1 and reject misinformation that conveys the impression that investing is complex.

Here are the primary strategies that support a more complicated view of investing:

1. **Rebalancing**
2. **Tax loss harvesting**
3. **Asset location**

None of these issues will likely have a meaningful impact on your returns. In any event, you can easily do them yourself.

Rebalancing Overview

Rebalancing refers to adjusting your portfolio's assets to maintain the desired level of risk and return.

Assume you have a portfolio with an allocation of 60% stocks and 40% bonds. Due to market gains, the value of the stocks in the portfolio increases significantly over time, causing the value of the stock portion of your portfolio to increase to 80% of the overall value.

Is It Necessary?

If you don't rebalance, you'll experience greater volatility and more significant unrealized losses when the market declines.

If those losses would cause you to panic and sell, you'll need to rebalance.

Here's why you may not want to rebalance. When you rebalance, you are selling assets that increased in value and buying assets that lost value. If you don't rebalance, your returns will likely increase since stocks have historically outperformed bonds over long periods.

Rebalancing may generate transaction fees and tax liability (unless the funds are in retirement accounts).

For these reasons, Jack Bogle's view on rebalancing was, "I'm in the small minority on the idea of rebalancing. I don't think you need to do it."

Do It Yourself

It's not necessary to resolve the debate over the merit of rebalancing. If you believe it's essential, it's easy to do it yourself.

To rebalance your portfolio, sell some of the increased value assets and use the proceeds to buy the underappreciated asset, returning the portfolio to its original allocation.

An easier way to rebalance would be to invest new contributions in the underappreciated asset until the correct asset allocation is restored.

Consider putting parameters on when you will rebalance. For example, if your target allocation is 60% stocks and 40% bonds, rebalance only when there's a 10% deviation. In this example, you would rebalance when your allocation of stocks drops to 50% or less or increases to 70% or more, at which time you would rebalance your portfolio to your target allocation of 60% stocks and 40% bonds.

Tax Loss Harvesting

Tax loss harvesting is a common strategy used in investing to minimize taxes. It involves selling securities that have experienced a loss and using those losses to offset any gains realized from other investments. Doing this can reduce your overall tax liability and increase your after-tax returns.

For many DIY investors, tax loss harvesting is unnecessary, primarily because most of their investments are in retirement or other tax-advantaged accounts. They have no tax liability until they withdraw those funds.

If you are married and filing jointly, you pay zero capital gains tax if your total taxable income in 2023 is $89,250 or below. If you are single, the taxable income amount is $44,625. If you fit into these categories, you don't need to engage in tax loss harvesting.

Even if you are in a higher income bracket, the amount of your capital gains tax may not justify tax loss harvesting. For example, if you are married and filing jointly, you can have a total taxable income between $89,251 and $553,850 and only pay a long-term capital gains tax of 15%. Tax loss harvesting makes the most sense for those in higher-income brackets.

For those investors, tax loss harvesting has the benefit of reducing your tax liability.

Here's another benefit: If your losses are larger than your gains, you can offset up to a maximum of $3000 of your ordinary taxable income and carry forward any amount over $3000 to future tax years, which reduces your taxable income.

Negatives of Tax Loss Harvesting

Tax loss harvesting has some downsides.

It may impact the risk level of your portfolio if it alters your asset allocation or have unintended tax consequences. For example, if the replacement stock you purchase increases significantly in value, you may incur an unexpected short-term gain greater than the loss you harvested.

Do It Yourself

While tax loss harvesting is more complicated than rebalancing, it's not beyond the competence of most DIY investors to do it themselves.

The steps involved are:

1. **Sell the losing investment.**
2. **Buy a similar investment, carefully avoiding running afoul of the "wash sale" rule. The easiest way to do this is to buy an ETF that targets similar stocks.**

A "wash sale" occurs when you sell a security at a loss to achieve tax benefits and promptly buy the same or similar security within 30 days before or after the sale.

If you need help, your CPA or a Certified Financial Planner who charges hourly may be a valuable resource. It should only take an hour or so of billable time.

Asset Location

Asset location is a strategy for optimizing after-tax returns by deciding which investments to hold in which types of accounts, like taxable accounts, tax-deferred retirement accounts (like 401(k)s and traditional IRAs), and tax-free retirement accounts (like Roth IRAs).

Is It Necessary?

For most millennials, asset location is not a concern.

Asset location strategies are generally only necessary if you hold a significant portion of your investments in taxable accounts, have diverse asset classes, and anticipate generating substantial capital gains from your portfolio.

If most of your savings are in tax-sheltered retirement accounts or your portfolio is modest, you don't need to be concerned about asset location.

Just because tax laws today favor specific asset locations doesn't mean those laws might not change in the future.

To do asset location properly, it's important to consider an investment's expected return and tax efficiency, which complicates the process considerably.

Guidelines for Asset Location

If you are in the minority of millennial investors who need to be concerned about asset location, here are some general guidelines:

- **Taxable accounts (brokerage accounts):** These accounts should generally be used for tax-efficient assets. Examples include index funds or ETFs (which tend to have lower turnover and thus generate fewer capital gain distributions), tax-managed funds, and individual stocks you plan to hold for a long time (where long-term capital gains rates apply). Municipal bonds, which generate tax-free interest, could also be held in these accounts if you are in a high tax bracket.
- **Tax-deferred accounts (401[k], Traditional IRA):** These are generally best for investments that generate a lot of taxable income, like bonds (other than municipal bonds), real estate investment trusts, and actively managed funds that may generate significant short-term capital gains.
- **Roth accounts:** Index funds and ETFs holding stocks may be well-suited for being held in a Roth account because capital gains and dividends generated with these accounts are tax-free when you make qualified withdrawals in retirement. If you hold stocks that pay dividends (like real estate investment trusts) or actively managed funds with high levels of turnover, your Roth is a good location for these investments.

Wealthier Tip

Many DIY investors don't need to be concerned with rebalancing, tax loss harvesting, or asset location. If these strategies are necessary, you can implement them yourself with modest effort.

Chapter 17
Ignore Naked Pundits

> *We find that none of the survey forecasts outperforms a simple random walk forecast, which predicts the future returns simply by their past sample mean.*
> —Songrun He, Jiaen Li, and Guofu Zhou, *How Accurate are Survey Forecasts on the Market?*

The stoic mindset embraces the present; Stoics recognized the unpredictability of the future. Seneca, an ancient Roman stoic philosopher, said, "The whole future lies in uncertainty. Live now, in the immediate present."

As a DIY investor, embrace this philosophy and ignore the bloviations of those engaged in predicting the future.

"Experts" Who Aren't

You turn on your favorite financial media channel. A distinguished-looking "expert" with impressive credentials discusses why their firm believes a particular company's stock is poised for significant growth.

Their reasoning seems logical and compelling and their views credible.

Here's the problem. They are emperors with no clothes.

They may be right or wrong about the stock. Tomorrow's news will determine the future price, but a pundit doesn't know what that will be. Relying on their musings offers you no better chance of picking a stock "winner" than a flip of a coin.

Your brain is tricking you into believing pundits have predictive powers.

The Forecasting Myth

Before delving into why your brain is predisposed to accept the views of pundits with no clothes, let's examine the forecasting myth.

Pundits love to make predictions about the direction of the market, the future stock price of a company, where interest rates are headed and other events that could impact investors.

Their ability to predict the future is no greater than random chance.

A recent academic study by three professors from the John M. Olin Business School of Washington University in St. Louis analyzed three widely used survey forecasts to determine how well they predicted the stock market. These surveys included economists from industry and academic institutions, U.S. financial professionals, and representative U.S. households.

The professional forecasters (which included highly trained economists) had a worse track record than the average household (you)!

In 2008, stocks fell 38.5%. Yet the median forecast from Wall Street "experts" predicted an 11.1% rise. The Wall Street consensus forecast was laughably wrong by 49.6 percentage points.

The Halo Effect

Accurate and reliable forecasting is a myth. Why do we believe in pundits with no clothes pretending to have expertise that doesn't exist?

When someone appears confident, well-dressed, and authoritative, it creates a positive impression that spills over to their perceived expertise. We believe people with these traits have abilities they can't substantiate (like the ability to predict future events).

This bias is called the Halo Effect.

It's well documented that we assign positive traits (like generosity, intelligence, and trustworthiness) to attractive people, even though there's no logical relationship between their appearance and those traits.

When we encounter people who match our mental image of experts, it impacts our brain and triggers the following reactions:

- **Reduced critical evaluation:** We may be more inclined to trust and accept their opinions and expertise without critically evaluating their arguments or considering alternative viewpoints.
- **Enhanced credibility:** Their opinions and statements may carry more weight and credibility.
- **Increased trust:** We may experience increased trust and be more confident in their knowledge and abilities, influencing our decision-making and willingness to follow their advice.
- **Emotional satisfaction:** Encountering individuals who match our mental image of experts can provide emotional satisfaction and reassurance, contributing to confidence and comfort.

These impressions are based on our perception, which may be superficial and misleading.

Availability Heuristic

We tend to overweight current information, which can cause us to ignore other pertinent facts. This tendency is called the "availability heuristic."

When an authoritative-looking "expert" urges us to change our investment portfolio, we may be inclined to make an emotional decision rather than calmly considering all relevant information.

To succeed as a DIY investor, you need to overcome this bias and stay the course.

Wealthier Tip

Understand the biases that may cause you to rely on the musings of pundits with no clothes.

Chapter 18
Don't Look for Patterns

Our brains are hardwired to see patterns in the world. It's why we cotton to lucky numbers, happy coincidences and all manner of reassuring "facts" that cannot be proven or even replicated.
—Mitch Tuchman, "Life on Mars? Money Tricks Our Brains Play," *Forbes*

Of all the mind tricks that impede your ability to succeed as a DIY investor, the most harmful is pattern-seeking.

Stoics were well aware of this issue. They rejected efforts to find "false patterns and foolish attempts to apply a single model to every problem you face."

You need to adopt this mindset with your investments.

Despite overwhelming evidence that stock prices are unpredictable, investors consistently use pattern detection and trend analysis to predict future market movements.

Our need to detect patterns may be evolutionary. Early humans relied on patterns like the behavior of animals, how the stars moved, and the changing seasons to survive. Recognizing patterns also helped them communicate, hunt, develop tools, develop cognitively, and advance culturally.

One study said their pattern-processing abilities became increasingly sophisticated as humans evolved. Finding patterns may be a primary reason humans are the dominant species.

Given this background, it's unsurprising that our brains are predisposed to find patterns—real or imagined.

Our Brain Seeks Patterns

It seems the brain *craves* patterns.

One study used functional MRI in a series of experiments. It found that when abstract symbols and patterns with no apparent similarity were shown to participants, it stimulated overlapping groups of neurons in their brains, suggesting a subconscious effort to group them.

We are well-equipped to find patterns even when they don't exist. We have a layer of our brains called the neocortex, which is only found in mammals. It accounts for 80% of the weight of the human brain. The neocortex includes an estimated 300 million neurons we use to identify patterns.

Our brains use this firepower to help us learn, predict, and determine probability. When it's misused to find nonexistent patterns, it can be harmful. In extreme cases, it can be a symptom of mental illness.

In the context of investing, it can be devastating.

Do You Have Apophenia?

Apophenia is "the perception of meaningful patterns in any unrelated information." In extreme situations, apophenia causes those with schizophrenia and autism to perceive excessive patterns, making it challenging to function.

In investing, apophenia takes various forms, all of which are harmful.

- You may see trends where none exist, like assuming a stock moving in a given direction will continue in that direction, even though those movements are random.
- You may perceive correlation where none exists, like associating a news event with a stock's price movement.
- You may extrapolate future events based on historical data and find a pattern that doesn't exist.
- You may believe unfounded conspiracies are impacting the stock market.

- You may believe a given investment is "due" for a downturn to compensate for its previous gains.

Just as in gambling, past events in the financial markets do not affect the probability of future events.

Combating Apophenia

You can start to combat apophenia by naming it.

If you say, "I am engaging in apophenia," there would be decreased activity in your brain's emotional centers, permitting the frontal lobe (the part of the brain that processes information rationally) to engage.

Focus on objective evidence and data rather than relying on intuition or gut feelings. Consider alternative explanations and perspectives rather than assuming a pattern.

The investment strategy recommended in Chapter 1 eliminates the need to find any patterns since you are buying the entire market and holding your investments for the long term.

Wealthier Tip

As a DIY investor, stop looking for patterns and focus instead on following sound investing principles.

III

112

Part Five
DIY Financial Planning

The pros, the cons, and the courage of entrepreneurs.

Chapter 19
Real Love

Chocolates get eaten and flowers wilt—but financial responsibility can be a lasting way to show someone you care.
— Fidelity, "4 Financial Ways to Say 'I love you,'"

I'll never forget meeting a widow whose husband died suddenly in his early sixties. She was a stay-at-home mom, and he dealt with their finances. He had done no estate planning and didn't have a will.

It took her months to determine how much money was in the estate. She wanted to know if she could afford to stay in her home, which they bought when they were first married.

I told her she would need to sell her home and should consider part-time employment to supplement her income.

She looked at me with tears in her eyes and said, "He always told me how much he loved me. I wonder if he did."

She's not alone.

Studies consistently show that, in marriages between a man and a woman, widows experience high rates of poverty due to income lost when their spouse dies.

You now have the tools to manage your investments. The ensuing chapters will show you how to engage in DIY financial planning for retirement. You have a moral duty to follow through.

Benefits of DIY Financial Planning

- **Protect their tomorrow:** We naturally seek to protect those we love by holding a child's hand as they cross the street or offering advice to a friend. Financial planning acts as this protective hand, but on a grander scale. It ensures your loved ones have a safety net, providing a buffer against unexpected challenges and hurdles when they need it the most.
- **Build together:** Whether sending your kids to college, buying your dream home, or planning for retirement, financial planning allows your dreams to flourish. Setting money aside or investing wisely means you're actively working toward making shared visions a reality.
- **Comfort and care:** Good health, quality education, and comfortable living are cornerstones of a happy life. With planning, you can make these values a reality for yourself and your loved ones now—and even after you're gone.
- **Leave a legacy:** Financial planning includes estate planning—ensuring that assets are passed down consistently with your wishes. Leaving a legacy shows a commitment to your family's well-being, even if you won't witness it. It's selfless and responsible.
- **Set an example:** When you prioritize financial planning, you impart a lesson to your loved ones about the importance of foresight, responsibility, and monetary wisdom. If you had the benefit of such an example, you can pass it on. If you didn't, you can begin a trend that impacts your family for generations.
- **Alleviate future burdens:** Debts, medical emergencies, or unplanned expenditures can strain relationships. By engaging in proactive financial planning, you reduce potential future burdens on your loved ones. It's an unspoken way of saying, "I've got this. I've got you."
- **Peace of mind:** Knowing your finances are in order and that there's a plan in place now and for the future brings peace of mind not just to you but to your entire family. It's the gift of restful nights and mornings that are greeted with hope rather than worry.

Love, in its purest form, is about the well-being of those dear to us. It's ensuring our shared future is woven with threads of security, comfort, and care.

Wealthier Tip

Planning your future together is the most profound, most authentic expression of your love.

Chapter 20

The Hype and the Reality

You will determine your financial goal based on some predictions and forecasts now. These forecasts and predictions might not hold in the future. They are subject to various conditions you might or might not consider. Thus, your financial plan might go for a toss if the predictions do not align with reality.

— TATA AIA, "What are the Advantages and Disadvantages of Financial Planning?"

Comprehensive financial planning is a process that helps you set, plan, and manage your long-term financial goals. Financial planning is undeniably crucial, yet it's more akin to an art than a science.

Comprehensive financial planning isn't math. There are too many unknown factors to make financial planning precise, including:

- Your life expectancy and the life expectancy of your spouse or partner
- The inflation rate over the planning period
- Your investment returns
- What tax laws and rates will be in the future
- Healthcare costs in the future
- Social Security and other government benefits
- Living expenses in retirement
- Lifestyle choices and your health in retirement
- Career changes
- Future interest rates
- Real estate values
- The need to support family members

- Economic and geopolitical factors
- Changes in laws affecting taxes and retirement accounts
- Unexpected disasters

The sheer number of assumptions makes retirement planning more of an informed guess than an exact science.

There are a range of outcomes for any financial plan. The three most sensitive inputs are income, spending and your desired retirement age.

The easiest factors to control are how long you will work and how frugally you will live.

Chart Your MONEY MAP

There's a simple, straightforward way to engage in DIY financial planning that I call crafting your "MONEY MAP." It aims to keep your plan simple, realistic, and focused on long-term success.

"M" is for Measure Your Cash Flow. Your cash flow needs regular attention. Monitoring what money you have coming in (like paychecks or side hustles) against what's going out (rent, groceries, gym membership), and making decisions accordingly, is crucial.

"O" is for Outline Your Goals. What do you want your finances to achieve for you? Getting out of debt? Buying a home? Make them SMART: Specific, Measurable, Achievable, Relevant, and Time-bound. Pin these goals to your mental or physical vision board as you chart a course to reach them.

"N" is for Net Worth. Your net worth is what you own minus what you owe. Calculate it by adding your assets (bank accounts, home, investments, and physical assets like your car) and then subtract your debts. Track it over time to see how you're doing. Are you getting financially "fitter?"

"E" is for Emergency Fund. Aim to save enough cash to cover three to six months of living expenses. You may need this fund to deal with unexpected expenses, like medical emergencies or the loss of a job.

"Y" is for Yield to a Budget. A budget is your personalized spending plan. Use budgeting tools to allocate your funds to splurge where it counts without sidelining your savings.

"M" is for Make Investment Choices. Invest intelligently, as outlined in Chapters 1 and 2.

"A" is for Assess Insurance Needs. Refer to the discussion of insurable risks in Chapter 31, life insurance in Chapter 32, and uninsurable risks in Chapter 33.

"P" is for Prepare for Retirement. Refer to Chapter 23 to calculate how much you will need.

Knowing all of this helps you understand where you are and how to get where you want to go. Your MONEY MAP isn't a static document. It should evolve as your life changes. Review and adapt it as you score new jobs, explore new relationships, or adjust your goals.

Wealthier Tip

Craft your MONEY MAP, your ultimate financial hack, to navigate the complexities of personal finance and transform them into a simple, actionable plan.

Chapter 21
Monte Carlo Analysis Can Be Misused

Why I advocate use of Monte Carlo analysis. 'I'd rather be vaguely right than precisely wrong.'
—Michael Kitces

Some financial planners extoll the ability of a "Monte Carlo analysis" to overcome the inherent unreliability of financial projections. It is a widely used tool in financial planning to assess potential outcomes over a specific time frame. It's often employed to calculate the probability of meeting retirement goals by considering current savings, anticipated contributions, investment returns, inflation, and withdrawal rates.

The term was coined by physicists trying to improve decision-making during World War II. It was named after the casino in Monaco because the element of chance is central to its modeling approach, "similar to a game of roulette."

Monte Carlo analysis was never intended to be a tool that brought mathematical precision to retirement planning.

An Overview of Monte Carlo Analysis

A Monte Carlo analysis simulates thousands of scenarios, providing a distribution of potential outcomes and helping clients gauge the likelihood of realizing their retirement goals.

A vital component of the analysis is to show how an investment portfolio will perform over time. The program considers asset allocation, historical market data, and volatility assumptions to generate simulated scenarios. By analyzing the resulting portfolio values, clients can supposedly evaluate the probability of achieving their investment objectives.

Monte Carlo analysis is also touted as helping evaluate the impact of potential risks in a financial plan. It can simulate market volatility, interest rate changes, unexpected expenses, income fluctuations, or scenarios like buying a house, starting a business, or changing career paths.

By quantifying the likelihood and potential magnitude of these risks and decisions, you can purportedly engage in risk mitigation strategies like insurance coverage, emergency funds, or adjusting investment allocations.

The result of the calculation is often expressed as a probability like, "You have a 95% probability of not outliving your money."

Monte Carlo Limitations

Despite the incredible computing power that generates a Monte Carlo analysis, the question persists—should you rely on it?

Much depends on the software used. What assumptions does it make about asset class returns, correlations, and other variables? Models may oversimplify or fail to capture all the complexities of real-world situations.

They can also suffer from biases. Inaccurate assumptions can lead to misleading outcomes. One study found that some models used in Monte Carlo analyses are more error-prone than others.

The quality of the output from Monte Carlo analysis is directly related to the quality of the input. If the underlying data for generating scenarios is flawed, the results will be similarly flawed.

Because a Monte Carlo analysis typically focuses on a specific set of variables and their distributions, it may overlook or inadequately account for unforeseen events, changes in market conditions, or external factors that can significantly impact investment performance.

There's also a problem with interpretation. You may believe a 90% chance of not running out of money is pretty good odds and do nothing to improve your situation. But what if you fall into the other 10%?

Notwithstanding its limitations, some respected experts believe a Monte Carlo analysis is a valuable way to derive insights from data and that it can be "a powerful tool for both market and risk analysis."

DIY Monte Carlo

If you believe a Monte Carlo analysis would aid your DIY financial planning, run one yourself.

The Portfolio Visualizer website offers a free Monte Carlo simulation tool that permits testing your expected portfolio growth and survival probability based on withdrawals.

Wealthier Tip

Before relying on the output of a Monte Carlo analysis, carefully consider its limitations.

Chapter 22
Entrepreneurial Courage

Whenever you see a successful business, someone once made a courageous decision.
—Peter F. Drucker

Almost 25 years ago, I met a remarkable man named Emery Kertesz. He was married with two young sons. He also had an incurable illness and knew he would likely die young.

He was dead broke and confronting the foreclosure of his home. While he was trained as an audio engineer, his illness made him unemployable.

It was the early days of the Internet. He came to me with an idea for an online venture selling audio equipment directly to businesses. He told me he would design and assemble the first product—ceiling speakers—in his garage to keep overhead down.

The venture capital he needed was within my reach.

I consulted with accountants and industry experts. They unanimously believed his idea was "a 100% loser." I ignored their advice and provided the funding based on a special feeling I had about Emery.

The business was modestly profitable from its first month of operation. Today, it's run by his sons and is flourishing.

Peter Drucker was right: It takes courage to start (or fund) a new business.

If you have the courage and can afford the risk, consider whether starting a business should be part of your DIY financial planning.

Millennials and Entrepreneurship

A 2020 study by GoDaddy of 3,000 Americans, including 1,000 millennials, found that 30% of millennials had a small business or side hustle. Almost 20% said it was their primary source of income.

The mindset of millennials is the primary reason this generation is so entrepreneurial. According to the study, "Forty-seven percent of millennials believe all Americans have the means to start their own business, and 84% revealed that they are more satisfied as an entrepreneur than when they worked for someone else."

Because of their technical expertise, millennials believe they are better suited to start a new business than prior generations.

The Entrepreneurial Mindset

Entrepreneurs are typically visionaries who see opportunities where others see challenges. They are willing to take calculated risks based on informed decisions. Setting goals as an entrepreneur means aligning your business vision with actionable steps and tangible milestones.

If you have started or want to start your own business, here's what you need to know about goal setting for entrepreneurship.

- **Incremental steps:** Entrepreneurs must balance their broad, strategic visions with the nitty-gritty of daily operations. This means setting overarching long-term goals that are broken down into shorter-term objectives. The long-term goal may be creating a market-leading product, while short-term goals include market research, product design, and initial prototype development.
- **Risk assessment:** The inherent risk in starting a business means goals must include risk assessment and contingency plans. Entrepreneurs often set challenging goals but have built-in flexibility to pivot as needed based on market feedback or financial reality.
- **Market research:** Before setting business goals, it's crucial to

understand your market and target demographic, so your goals reflect what customers need.
- **Evaluate the competition:** Goals should also consider the competitive landscape. This includes evaluating competitors and identifying unique selling propositions for your business.
- **Financial projections:** One of the primary goals for any new business is securing startup capital. Goals around funding include pitching to investors, applying for loans or grants, or launching a crowdfunding campaign.
- **Budgeting:** Financial goal setting involves detailed budgeting and setting clear revenue targets. These goals are not only crucial for the viability of the business but also for attracting investors who need to see a path to profitability.
- **Legal and regulatory compliance:** Setting up a new business involves consideration of legal and regulatory issues, including the form of corporate entity you will establish, understanding tax obligations, and obtaining necessary licenses and permits.
- **Intellectual property:** Entrepreneurs need to protect their intellectual property, including filing for patents, trademarks, or copyrights.
- **Marketing:** Marketing and brand development are crucial goals for any new business. This could include designing a logo, developing a brand voice, and creating a marketing strategy that aligns with the values of the business and the target demographic.
- **Engagement strategies:** Engagement strategies include website development, social media strategy, and content marketing to engage potential customers and build a community around the brand.
- **Planning for growth:** Entrepreneurs should set goals for scalability. Set up systems and processes to handle an increase in volume, and consider potential future markets.
- **Monitoring progress:** Entrepreneurs need to evaluate success. This means establishing key performance indicators (KPIs) and regularly reviewing processes to assess what's working and what needs adjustment.
- **Personal development:** Entrepreneurial goals include the founder's personal development, especially enhancing leadership skills, learning about new market trends, and acquiring specific industry knowledge.
- **Team building:** Build a capable team beginning with the first employee hired. Identify critical roles within the company and create a culture that attracts top talent.

- **Be nimble:** Entrepreneurs need to be nimble. Your business environment can change rapidly, and successful entrepreneurs must be willing to change their goals in response to new information or market shifts.

Entrepreneurship is a unique landscape where goals aren't just aspirations but the building blocks of your future enterprise. By incorporating these considerations into goal-setting practices, you will maximize your chances for success and justify your courageous decision to start your company.

Wealthier Tip

While starting a business involves significant risk, careful goal setting and related planning can maximize the possibility of success.

Part Six
Getting to "the Number"

It may not be
as much—or as
difficult—
as you think.

Chapter 23
How Much is Enough?

One of the traditional rules of thumb about how much you should save for retirement is the 4 percent rule. The idea here is that you should draw down no more than 4 percent of your retirement accounts in a given year, so that you can make your assets last over your retirement.
—James Royal, Ph.D. and Brian Baker, CFA, "How much should I save for retirement?," *Bankrate*

Here's a critical question you'll need to address: How much will you need to retire and maintain your quality of life without running out of money during your and your loved ones' lives?

It can feel like an unknowable or insurmountable amount, but it's not. Don't let fear or inertia overwhelm and keep you from making the simple, proactive choices that will lead to the life you want.

The financial media wants you to believe you must earn a fortune to accumulate enough to retire, but that's not always true. Your income alone doesn't determine your financial destiny.

Olive Swindells died at 94 with a $4.4 million stock portfolio. Her husband was a draftsman. There were no other apparent sources of income. They lived in a modest home and invested in a stock portfolio that flourished over the years.

Ronald Read was a retired gas station attendant and janitor. When he died in 2015, he left an estate worth $8 million. He lived frugally, held his investments for a long time, and benefited from compounding over a long life.

Strong retirement planning is about balancing wealth accumulation with enjoying your life in the present.

Factors to Consider in Retirement Planning

Almost everyone wants to maintain their standard of living during retirement. This goal can seem daunting because you have to plan to deal with increased healthcare costs and the erosion of your purchasing power due to inflation. Other considerations include:

- "Longevity risk." No one wants to outlive their money.
- When you can retire and how much you can withdraw each year to ensure that your savings last throughout your retirement.
- Emergencies, unforeseen expenses, and perhaps fulfilling your desire to leave a legacy to children or grandchildren.

The endgame of planning is knowing how much is "enough." Once you have that number, you can plan to reach it. Knowing how much is enough can provide financial peace of mind, diminish the fear of running out of money, and reduce anxiety about market fluctuations. If your "enough" number requires a higher rate of return on your investments, you may need to accept a higher level of volatility.

To find out your number, you need to understand your financial goals (and how much they will cost) and align that knowledge with your investment strategy. It differs from person to person depending on, risk tolerance, lifestyle choices, and retirement plans.

Finding Your "Enough" Number

If it's so important, why do so few people know their "enough" number, and why do even fewer have a plan for achieving it?

Here are some basic guidelines that are easy to follow.

According to Fidelity, you'll need to save ten times your preretirement income by age 67 to ensure sufficient income to maintain your quality of life in retirement.

While 15 to 20% (depending on your age when you start saving) is a recommended savings rate, adjusting this percentage to your specific circumstances is important.

You may need to alter your savings rate if you have high debt levels or other financial obligations (see the discussion of consumer smoothing in Chapter 26).

Fidelity estimates you should plan to spend between 55 and 80% of your annual working income every year throughout retirement. The exact amount will depend on your retirement lifestyle and healthcare costs. The percentage you will spend varies depending on your quality of life in retirement and your income level.

Rather than calculating the amount you need to save based on your current income, consider shifting the focus to your expenses. In retirement, you will need to cover your expenses, not necessarily match your preretirement income.

Calculate how much you are currently spending and assume it will increase annually by the historical rate of inflation.

While 3.8% was the average inflation rate from 1960-2022, over the past decade inflation has averaged only 1.88%. If you believe the Federal Reserve is managing inflation differently and the past decade is more representative of the future, consider using a less conservative inflation rate, like 3.00%. You could also use a lower number for general inflation and a higher one for healthcare and education expense, since those areas are long-term drivers of higher inflation.

Other factors to consider when you apply these guidelines to your unique situation:

Life expectancy (for you and your spouse): The good news is that Americans are living longer than previous generations. On the flip side, you must plan to avoid running out of money as you age.

The Social Security Administration has a "Retirement & Survivors Benefits: Life Expectancy Calculator" on its website. Select your gender, enter your date of birth, and it will calculate the average number of additional years you can expect to live.

While this calculator helps provide an estimate, it isn't customized. It doesn't consider advancements in healthcare, changes in lifestyle, socioeconomic status, and individual circumstances, all of which can influence life expectancy.

You could get a customized life expectancy estimate using "The Living to 100 Life Expectancy Calculator." This calculator is based on The New England Centenarian

Study, the most comprehensive study of centenarians and their families. It asks 40 questions about your health and family history and only takes about ten minutes to complete. After you answer the questions, you'll receive personalized feedback.

Current annual income: Assume your income will increase by the rate of inflation.

Expected rate of return on investments: You will need to rely on historical data to input the expected rate of return on your investments. Unfortunately, historical returns don't guarantee future performance. Market conditions and economic factors can vary significantly, and the performance of stocks and bonds can fluctuate. Returns are often expressed as "average annualized returns," assuming level returns over time, which is not what happens. See the discussion of sequence of returns in Chapter 25.

Your asset allocation plays a significant role in determining future expected returns. The expected returns of a portfolio with a higher percentage of stocks will be greater than one allocated primarily to bonds.

If this seems overwhelming, consider using a retirement calculator which will give you good approximation.

Wealthier Tip

By following some general guidelines, DIY retirement planners may be able to get as reliable an estimate of how much they will likely need to sustain their lifestyle in retirement as they could using sophisticated software.

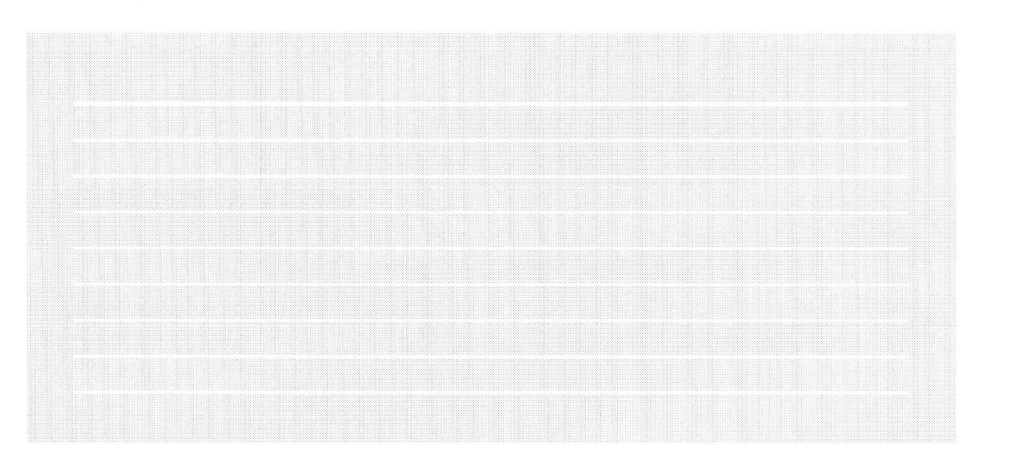

Chapter 24
The Role of Gratitude

> *It's often said that if you have food in your fridge, clothes on your back, and roof over your head to sleep under, you are richer than 75% of the world.*
>
> —Justin Chidester, *"How Gratitude Helps You Retire Early," Wealth Mode*

The securities industry has an economic interest in making you believe you must save vast amounts of money for retirement. That belief generates fees and commissions that pad their bottom line.

How much do *you* need to be happy in retirement?

When answering that question, don't overlook the critical role of gratitude.

Stoics understood the relationship between wanting less and increased gratitude. The stoic view of gratitude was summarized by Marcus Aurelius: "All you need are these: certainty of judgment in the present moment; action for the common good in the present moment; and an attitude of gratitude in the present moment for anything that comes your way."

The Impact of Gratitude

In 2003, a study co-authored by Robert A. Emmons and Michael E. McCullough, published in the *Journal of Personality and Social Psychology*, investigated the role of gratitude and subjective well-being in daily life. It found that participants who were instructed to focus on the parts of their lives for which they were grateful experienced "heightened well-being."

An article in *The New York Times* summarized the study and quoted Dr. Emmons: "Gratitude heals, energizes and changes lives... It is the prism through which we view life in terms of gifts, givers, goodness, and grace."

Other studies have found that practicing gratitude is associated with lower blood pressure and other positive changes in health metrics.

Practicing gratitude can help make retirement—and your life today—more enjoyable and fulfilling without costing you a dime. When you take time to appreciate the people, experiences, and blessings in your life, it cultivates positive emotions and reduces feelings of boredom or dissatisfaction.

Here's how practicing gratitude can reduce the amount of money needed in retirement:

- By focusing on gratitude, you shift your mindset from accumulating more to appreciating what you have. Doing so can lead to living a more modest lifestyle and needing less.
- Gratitude helps you value relationships and experiences over material items, leading to less spending.
- Expressing gratitude reduces stress and anxiety, resulting in better health and lower medical costs.
- Appreciating life's simple joys like nature, friends, and hobbies can fill your time in retirement with little cost.
- A grateful mindset increases self-esteem and resilience, making it easier to adapt to financial changes in retirement.
- Gratitude makes you less likely to overspend on wants versus needs, increasing contentment.
- Grateful people often want to give back. Finding meaning by volunteering time or donating to causes can lead to needing less income.

Challenges to Contentment

I don't mean to minimize the challenges of being content with less. From a psychological and neuroscientific perspective, the perpetual quest for more—material possessions, achievements, or experiences—is programmed into our brains. That's part of the reason why gratitude needs to be a deliberate practice.

The Hedonic Treadmill and Adaptation-Level theories offer perspective on how we adapt to positive or negative life changes and how that impacts our happiness levels.

The Hedonic Treadmill theory states that we have a baseline level of happiness that we eventually return to after experiencing positive or adverse events. Someone who wins the lottery or gets a big promotion may experience a temporary boost in happiness. But over time, they will adapt to their new circumstances and return to their original happiness set point.

On the hedonic treadmill, you constantly strive for more pleasure but never feel satisfied.

Staying on the hedonic treadmill is expensive. Practicing gratitude is free.

The Adaptation-Level theory, developed by psychologist Harry Helson, suggests that we adapt to stimuli and experiences over time. Our adaptation level adjusts as positive or negative events occur, but eventually, we get used to our new normal.

Here's an example: You walk into a bakery and are immediately overwhelmed by the smell of freshly baked goods. After waiting in line for a few minutes, your awareness disappears, even though the level of scent is the same. You have adapted to the new stimuli.

These two theories suggest that positive or negative changes don't permanently impact our happiness. We experience short-term fluctuations based on life events but ultimately revert to our baseline. Therefore, we can't rely on major external events, possessions, or achievements to dramatically impact our long-term happiness.

Neuroscience offers another explanation for why we believe material possessions will increase our happiness. As discussed in Chapter 14, dopamine is released when we experience something new or engage in pleasurable activities, like running a marathon or achieving a personal goal.

A problem occurs when we adapt to the levels of dopamine released by particular achievements or possessions. We may then require more significant accomplishments or possessions to trigger the same level of pleasure, leading to a never-ending chase for more.

Social comparison theory is a psychological concept that explains how we evaluate ourselves by comparing our abilities, beliefs, and opinions with others. The theory posits that we have an innate drive to evaluate ourselves compared to others.

Social media exacerbates social comparison. The lives presented online may lead to unrealistic comparisons, amplifying feelings of inadequacy and dissatisfaction.

When we continuously compare ourselves to others we perceive as living superior lives, we feel inadequate or less successful, reducing self-esteem and reinforcing a sense of failure, impacting our overall happiness.

Social comparison often leads to a desire for more material possessions to "keep up" with others. This pursuit of material wealth can become an endless cycle that detracts from true contentment and fulfillment.

Understanding the interplay of these ideas shifts baseline satisfaction from acquiring more material goods to practices like gratitude, mindfulness, strong relationships, and finding purpose.

Wealthier Tip

Quenching the thirst for "more" means shifting our focus to more meaningful aspects of our lives.

Chapter 25
A Trap for the Unwary

> *The average market return over a thirty-year period could be quite generous. But if negative returns are experienced when you start spending from your portfolio, you will face an insurmountable hurdle that cannot be overcome even if the market offers higher returns later in retirement.*
>
> —Wade Pfau, Ph.D., CFA, RICP®, "Navigating One of The Greatest Risks of Retirement Income Planning," *Retirement Researcher*

When evaluating your "enough" number, you should consider sequence of returns because it could have a meaningful impact on your quality of life in retirement.

Sequence of returns is the order in which investment returns occur over a period of time. It is an important concept in financial planning, particularly retirement planning because the timing and order of investment returns can significantly impact your overall portfolio value if you are contributing to or withdrawing from your portfolio.

Paying attention to your asset allocation and your withdrawals during retirement can prevent significant disruptions.

Why Sequence Matters

Let's use the S&P 500 index as an example.

The average annualized return of the S&P 500 index since its inception in 1926 is 10.13%. This data may cause you to believe you can count on consistent returns of 10.13% yearly, which isn't the case.

If you look at the index's actual returns for each year since 1926, you may be surprised to learn they vary wildly. For example, in 2008, the index lost 37% of its value, and in 2019, it gained 31.49%.

This variation can impair the sustainability of a portfolio in the withdrawal phase.

When investment returns are positive early in retirement, your portfolio can grow and offset potential losses in later years. However, if negative returns occur early in retirement, it can significantly deplete the value of your portfolio, making it difficult to recover even if positive returns follow.

In this example provided by Charles Schwab, two investors each have a portfolio of $1 million. They each withdraw $50,000 per year (adjusted for inflation). Both experience a 15% decline in portfolio value, but at different times.

Investor 1 suffers the decline in the first two years of retirement.

Investor 2 suffers the same decline in the 10th and 11th years of retirement.

In the 18th year of retirement, Investor 1 runs out of money. Investor 2 still has a portfolio worth $400,000.

Managing Sequence of Returns Risk

Managing sequence of returns risk is challenging.

You could reduce withdrawals in down years.

You might consider tapping into your home equity and the cash value of life insurance during these times so you don't have to withdraw from your portfolio.

You could increase the amount of your emergency fund and use it during periods of negative stock returns.

Maintain a reserve of liquid investments (like short-term bond funds, short-term Certificates of Deposit and money market accounts) you can use to pay expenses without selling stocks at a loss.

The potential threat of sequence of returns risk shows the importance of ensuring your asset allocation—particularly the amount allocated to bonds—is appropriate for your risk tolerance. Taking distributions from your bonds will protect you against selling stocks in a down market but may leave you with a more volatile portfolio.

Wealthier Tip

Pay attention to sequence of returns before and during retirement to avoid a catastrophic impact on your quality of life.

Chapter 26
Smoothing Over Savings

Regardless of the amount you save, you will definitely be in a better situation if you start early than if you wait until your mid-30s or 40s.

—Jack VanDerhei, Research Director of the Employee Benefits Research Institute

Just about every financial book extolls the virtues of saving early. The premise for this advice is irrefutable. Saving early harnesses the power of compound interest.

The following true story illustrates the power of compound interest.

Grace Groner was orphaned at age 12. Family friends raised her and her twin sister.

After graduation from Lake Forest College in 1931, she was employed as a secretary for Abbott Laboratories, where she remained for over four decades.

In her first year of employment, she purchased three shares of Abbott stock for $60 each and held that stock for the rest of her life.

She lived frugally in a small one-bedroom cottage. When her car was stolen, she didn't buy another one and walked instead.

When she passed away in 2010 at 100, her investment was worth $7.2 million. In addition to her frugal lifestyle, this incredible result was due to stock splits, appreciation in the value of her shares, and the power of compound interest. The dividends in her Abbott stock were reinvested to buy more shares, generating more dividends, which she used to buy more shares.

Don't take the wrong lesson from this story. I'm not recommending you purchase an individual stock and hope for results similar to what Ms. Groner achieved. But her inspirational story demonstrates the power of living below your means, the stunning impact of compound interest and the benefit of engaging in "masterly inactivity" (as discussed in Chapter 15).

A famous illustration of compound interest is the fable of the chessboard and the grain of rice.

The inventor of chess presented his chessboard to the emperor of India. The emperor was duly impressed and told him to name a price as a reward for his ingenuity.

The man responded, "Oh, Emperor, my wishes are simple. I only wish for this. Give me one grain of rice for the first square of the chessboard, two grains for the next square, four for the next, eight for the next and so on for all 64 squares, with each square having double the number of grains as the square before."

Initially, the emperor was struck by this modest request but after one week, he realized he couldn't meet it.

Here's why: "...on the 64th square, the king would have had to put more than 18,000,000,000,000,000,000 grains of rice, which is equal to about 210 billion tons. It is sufficient to cover the whole territory of India with a meter-thick layer of rice."

That's the magic of compound interest.

Barriers to Saving Early

Saving early harnesses this power and is a great idea...if you can do it. Starting as early as possible at a consistent savings rate ranging from 10% to 20% of income would be ideal.

There are three problems with this advice:

1. **It doesn't take into consideration the amount already saved.**
2. **It doesn't account for the ability to save more based on salary increases.**
3. **It doesn't consider the inability of younger people to meet this savings goal.**

The third issue is particularly troublesome. For many millennials, making ends meet in the early years of employment is challenging, and then later the feeling of already being behind is demotivating.

A More Realistic Approach

Economists offer another approach, the Life Cycle Hypothesis (LCH).

LCH is an economic theory developed by economist Franco Modigliani and his student Richard Brumberg in the 1950s that seeks to explain spending and saving patterns over a lifetime.

The premise of LCH is that we shift our focus from a consistent savings rate to "smoothing" our consumption level ("consumption smoothing"). LCH assumes wealth accumulation follows a "hump-shaped" pattern, which results in little or no savings in early years (and even taking on debt during those years) and maximizes savings in years when earnings are the highest.

Consumption smoothing is controversial. Some financial experts believe it encourages incurring debt and excessive spending at a young age and ignores how quickly we adapt to increased income. These concerns are valid if consumption smoothing is interpreted as encouraging profligate debt at a young age.

A more practical approach would be to live frugally and avoid as much debt as possible while young. Then exercise discipline to live well below your means as your income increases, permitting higher savings rates at that time.

The *White Coat Investor* advises, "Start your life with very frugal habits, and you will always feel wealthy."

Ditch Guilt

Traditional fixed savings rate advice can make you feel guilty if you're saddled by student loan debt, were impacted by the Great Recession of 2008, harmed by the COVID-19 pandemic, or are otherwise unable to save during your early years.

You're not alone, and your retirement goals have not been irreparably harmed.

Shift your focus from a rigid savings goal to smoothing your consumption over your lifespan. Doing so will permit you to save more when you earn more and compensate for times you weren't as able to save.

Wealthier Tip

While starting to save early is optimal, if it's not possible, shift your focus to smoothing your consumption and saving more when you earn more.

Chapter 27
Modern Budgeting

Having a goal in mind for your budget is important when you decide how much money to set aside and how much to spend.
—Yale University, "Budgeting and Goal Setting, Financial Literacy"

You know you need a budget, but it's very low on your list of priorities.

Goal setting without budgeting is like trying to sail a ship without a map or compass. You might eventually get somewhere, but you're more likely to get lost along the way.

The modern workforce, defined by technological advancements, the gig economy, and a shift in career and life values, confronts a different financial landscape compared to older generations. These changes require a reevaluation of budgeting strategies.

- **Retirement:** Today, the responsibility of retirement planning often falls entirely on individuals who must budget for contributions to retirement accounts like 401(k)s and IRAs, without the cushion of a pension.
- **Healthcare:** Previously, comprehensive healthcare benefits were a common perk provided by employers, which minimized individual healthcare costs. With the rise of high-deductible health plans and the gig economy, many employees need to budget for higher out-of-pocket healthcare expenses.
- **HSAs and FSAs:** To manage higher healthcare costs, modern workers eligible for Health Savings Accounts and Flexible Spending Accounts should consider contributing to these accounts, which offer tax advantages for medical expenses.

- **Technology:** Modern budgeters have the advantage of financial technology. Apps like You Need a Budget (YNAB), and Empower (formerly Personal Capital) can help track variable income and expenses, set financial goals, and monitor investments. Apps like PocketGuard track spending "to help customers spend less than they earn."
- **Dynamic Spending:** Historical budgets suggested allocating 50% of income toward needs, 30% toward wants, and 20% toward savings and debt repayment. This formula might need tweaking for the modern workforce that adopts a more dynamic approach where percentages fluctuate monthly based on income and expenses.
- **Continuous Learning:** Continuous learning and upskilling should be part of a modern budget. Given the rapid pace of change in job markets, setting aside funds for professional development is an investment in financial stability.
- **Debt Management:** With the potential for income variability, a solid debt repayment plan is essential. This might involve strategies like the debt snowball approach (pay off the smallest debt first; make the minimum payment on others) or the avalanche method (pay off highest interest debt first; make the minimum payment on others).

While the foundational principles of budgeting remain constant—spend less than you earn, save for the future, and live within your means—applying these principles has evolved with the times.

Wealthier Tip

Budgeting is a critical component of financial planning. Make sure your budget accounts for the realities of modern life.

Chapter 28
Slay Student Loans

Millions of Americans are affected by the burden of student loan debt. In the United States, student loan debt is nearing $2 trillion.
—California Department of Financial Protection & Innovation

When you're saddled with student loan debt, it's challenging to plan for the future.

More than 45 million former students are carrying student loan debt. Almost half of them still owe over $20,000 twenty years after starting school. The average debt is $37,338 per borrower. Private student loan debt is even higher at $54,921 per borrower.

In addition to repaying the principal, interest is a major factor in student debt. Almost 92% of student loan debt is federal, charging interest rates ranging from 4.99% to 7.54%. Private student loan rates can top out at nearly 15%.

If you're facing student loan debt, it's easy to feel hopeless, but don't give up on your long-term goals. Below are strategies for managing this debt.

Knowledge is Power

If you have a federal loan, go to the Federal Student Aid website and confirm your understanding of the loan amounts, interest rates, and repayment terms for each loan. Do the same with your private loan servicer if you have a private loan.

It might feel depressing to look at the numbers, but having an accurate sense of where you stand is critical to making a plan to meet your goals.

Loan Forgiveness and Payment Plans

Some borrowers qualify for loan forgiveness. If this applies to you, it's a no-brainer to opt in. The Federal Student Aid website lists all the categories that qualify for loan forgiveness—the most common being the Public Service Loan Forgiveness program.

Lesser-known possibilities include a loan discharge under certain circumstances if your school closed or misled you.

Efforts by the federal government to forgive student loan debt are ongoing. You should monitor these developments to see if you qualify.

Whether you're on the path to loan forgiveness or not, the U.S. Education Department has implemented an affordable student loan repayment plan called "Saving on a Valuable Education" (SAVE).

Highlights of the SAVE plan include a payment cap of 5% of discretionary income (as defined) for those with undergraduate loans, a reduction in monthly interest for interest not covered by income-driven adjustments, and loan forgiveness if original balances were $12,000 or less after 120 payments have been made.

Pay It Off Early

For most DIY investors, paying off their student loan debt early makes sense, especially if you don't qualify for a tax deduction for your student loan interest. If you hold several student loans, pay off the ones with the highest interest first.

If you hold non-student-loan debt with higher interest rates, consider paying off that debt first.

See if Your Employer Can Help

The Consolidated Appropriations Act of 2023 can help reduce student loan debt by permitting employers to give employees up to $5,250 in tax-exempt student loan repayment assistance through January 1, 2026. Employers can deduct these payments as a business expense, and employees can exclude them from their income. It's a win-win.

Starting in 2024, the Secure 2.0 Act of 2023, part of the Consolidated Appropriations Act of 2023, will allow employers to make matching contributions to their 401(k) plans for employees making "qualified higher education loan repayments."

Ask your employer if they have a student loan contribution program in place.

Consider Refinancing

If you can refinance your federal loan into a private loan at a lower interest, think carefully before taking this step. If you refinance, a private lender will hold your new loan, not the U.S. government. You won't be eligible for future loan moratoriums, loan reduction, or forgiveness programs available to those holding federal loans.

If you hold a private student loan, consider refinancing or consolidating after running the numbers and deciding that the savings on interest or the difference in other terms (like shortening the term or removing a co-signer) warrants the effort.

Wealthier Tip

Take advantage of government and employer programs to minimize and pay off your debt. Prioritize paying off loans so that you can shift your focus to your long-term goals.

Chapter 29
Tax Tricks

Tax planning is the analysis and arrangement of a person's financial situation in order to maximize tax breaks and minimize tax liabilities in a legal and efficient manner.
—Sabrina Parys and Tina Orem, "Tax Planning for Beginners: 6 Tax Strategies and Concepts to Know," *Nerdwallet*

Tax planning helps you keep more of what you make. That means you have more control of your money and can better use it to live the life you want.

If your financial life is straightforward, you may be able to go it alone. Otherwise, you'll probably need the assistance of a Certified Public Accountant (CPA) or a financial advisor who is also a CPA.

Characterizing the U.S. federal tax code a complex labyrinthine and interminable is an understatement. It's about 2,600 pages and well over one million words. When you add IRS regulations, revenue rulings, clarifications, court decisions, notations, and other information, you reach 70,000 pages. It changes every year.

What is Tax Planning?

Tax planning is a strategy to minimize tax liability by taking advantage of deductions, credits, and exemptions. Tax planning is *really* important and impacts your financial planning in the following ways:

- **Reduces tax liability:** Tax planning helps you legally minimize your tax burden. By incorporating tax planning into your financial decisions, you pay less tax, allowing you to keep more of your hard-earned money.
- **Maximizes income:** By strategically structuring financial transactions and investments, you can retain more earnings, allowing you to save,

invest, or spend on your priorities.
- **Avoiding penalties and interest:** Failing to plan for taxes appropriately can result in penalties and interest.
- **Asset protection:** Some tax planning strategies (like establishing a trust) can help protect your assets from potential creditors.
- **Peace of mind:** Knowing you have a well-thought-out tax plan can provide peace of mind and remove uncertainties about tax obligations, allowing for better financial planning and reduced stress during tax season.
- **Estate planning:** Proper estate planning can help minimize the tax burden on heirs and preserve more of your estate's value.
- **Adapts to changing tax laws:** Tax laws change. Tax planning allows you to adapt to these changes while staying within legal boundaries.
- **Investment strategies:** Tax planning considerations can significantly impact investment decisions. Understanding the tax implications of different investment options allows you to make more informed choices.

Common tax planning strategies you may be able to use to minimize your tax burden include:

- **Maximize deductions and credits:** Tax deductions reduce your taxable income and lower your tax liability. "Above the line" deductions reduce your income (e.g., pre-tax contributions to a retirement account). "Below the line" deductions reduce your adjusted gross income (e.g., mortgage interest).
  Each year, you can take either a standard deduction (in the amount set by the IRS) or itemize your deductions.
  A tax credit is a dollar-for-dollar reduction of the income tax you owe the IRS (e.g., using solar panels on your home).
  Identify and claim all eligible deductions and tax credits. Using a qualified tax professional or tax software can help ensure you don't miss any.
- **Use tax-advantaged accounts:** Contributing to tax-advantaged accounts like Individual Retirement Accounts (IRAs), 401(k)s, or Health Savings Accounts (HSAs) can help lower taxable income and grow investments tax-free or tax-deferred. Roth IRAs will permit your money to grow tax-free. You can generally make tax-free withdrawals after age 59½.
- **Time income and expenses:** Shifting the timing of income and expenses from one tax year to another can affect tax liability. For example, deferring a year-end bonus to the following year or prepaying certain deductible expenses before year-end can minimize tax liability.

- **Charitable contributions:** Making tax-deductible donations to qualified charities can reduce taxable income. Donor-advised funds can be a simple, flexible and tax-advantageous way to contribute to charity.
- **Tax-efficient investment strategies:** Investments with preferential tax treatment, like municipal bonds, can reduce your overall tax burden.
- **Business structures:** If you are self-employed, choosing the proper business structure (e.g., sole proprietorship, partnership, LLC, S corporation) can have significant tax implications.
- **Tax-efficient withdrawal strategies:** For retirees, planning the timing and sources of retirement withdrawals can help minimize taxes.

Choosing Professionals

Because of the importance and complexity of tax planning, you will likely require a CPA. Qualifications and characteristics to consider when hiring one:

- **CPA Designation:** The most basic requirement is that the professional is a Certified Public Accountant, meaning they have passed a rigorous examination and met the specific licensing requirements of their state. You can verify the status of a CPA on the website CPAverify.
- **Tax specialization:** Look for someone who specializes in tax planning and preparation. Some CPAs may have more experience with corporate tax, auditing, or accounting rather than individual tax planning.
- **Continuing education:** Tax laws are constantly changing, so it's important to find a CPA who prioritizes staying current on the latest tax legislation and can advise you accordingly.
- **Professional memberships:** Membership in professional bodies like the American Institute of CPAs (AICPA) can indicate a commitment to ethical behavior and ongoing education. Some CPAs might also have a Personal Financial Specialist (PFS) credential.
- **Communication skills:** Since tax laws can be complex, choose a CPA who communicates clearly.
- **Affordability:** Make sure you understand their fees.

WEALTHIER TIP

Consult a CPA to ensure you are implementing the best tax strategies for your situation and goals.

Chapter 30
Shortfalls

The baby boomers worked so hard during their careers, and they feel now is the time to enjoy themselves. They have a hard time saying no to travel, gifts to kids and grandkids, and are spending too much. They need to have a plan B to fall back on when their savings start to diminish.

—Jessica Weaver, financial advisor and author, quoted in "6 Ways to Fix a Retirement Savings Shortfall," by Jeff Brown, *US News*

Avoiding the retirement savings mistakes of your parents is a crucial goal for millennials as you plan for your financial future.

By starting to save as early as possible, engaging in consumer smoothing, contributing to retirement accounts, and creating and sticking to a budget, you can build a solid foundation for a secure retirement.

Maintaining a balance between supporting family members, safeguarding retirement savings, and continuously educating yourself about finances helps you make prudent financial decisions and avoid the challenges previous generations have faced.

Catching Up

If you find yourself saving the maximum amount you can but still need to catch up to accumulate the funds you'll need for retirement, there are several steps you can take to improve your situation.

- **Increase your exposure to stocks.** You may need to increase the allocation of stocks in your portfolio, which will increase your expected returns. The flip side is that the volatility of your portfolio will be higher,

as will the depth of your losses in a down market.
- **Reduce expenses.** Identify areas where you can reduce discretionary spending and allocate the difference toward retirement savings.
- **Increase your income.** Explore ways to earn additional income through a side venture, taking on extra work, negotiating a raise at your current job, or changing jobs.
- **Revisit your retirement goals.** Assess whether your retirement goals are realistic, given your current financial circumstances. You may need to adjust your expectations or consider working longer to accumulate the necessary funds.
- **Reduce debt.** If you have high-interest debt (like credit card debt), pay it down as quickly as possible. Eliminating or reducing this debt will free up more money for retirement savings.
- **Downsize or relocate.** Consider whether downsizing your home or relocating to an area with a lower cost of living might be feasible. If you can reduce your housing expenses, you will free up additional savings funds.
- **Rent a room.** If zoning regulations permit, consider renting a room or section of your home.

Get Creative

While the traditional ways of catching up are tried and true, there are also out-of-the-box suggestions that can increase your long-term savings.

Move to a tiny house. Moving into a tiny home could dramatically decrease costs associated with property taxes, utilities, maintenance, and repairs. With less space to fill, you'll also save on material goods. The average cost of a tiny house ranges from $30,000–$60,000, which doesn't include the land cost.

A tiny home requires a significant adjustment. You would need to be comfortable with a minimalist lifestyle and be willing to let go of possessions that don't fit in your reduced space.

There may also be zoning restrictions or community regulations to navigate.

Move to a lower cost-of-living country. It's expensive to retire in the United States, which has the world's tenth-highest cost of living.

According to *U.S.News*, you can "embrace a high standard of living" in the following cities for as little as $1,000 a month:

- Chiang Rai, Thailand
- Corozal, Belize
- Cuenca, Ecuador
- Granada, Nicaragua
- Medellín, Columbia
- Tagaytay, The Philippines
- Kyrenia, Northern Cyprus
- Chitré, Panama

While the appeal of improving your quality of life while reducing your costs is obvious, making this massive change in your life has serious downsides:

- You will be far from family and friends.
- You may encounter political instability.
- You'll need to research healthcare standards and costs carefully.
- There are costs involved in transportation, buying or leasing a place to live, and moving your belongings.
- You may be subject to taxation in the country of your new residence and the U.S.
- You may incur expensive fees in transferring funds from the U.S. to your new country of residence.
- You may have difficulty adapting to a new culture and language.

The key to a successful retirement is planning early, anticipating any shortfall, and dealing with it realistically and perhaps creatively.

Wealthier Tip

The earlier you identify a shortfall in your retirement savings, the more options you will have to deal with it.

154

Part Seven
A Twist on Risk

Risk reduction
at a discount.

Chapter 31
Insurable Risks

> *Risk management for individuals is a critical element of life-cycle finance. It recognizes that as investors age, the fundamental nature of their total wealth evolves, as do the risks they face.*
> — CFA Institute, "Risk Management for Individuals"

The risks we confront in life can be overwhelming. The critical first step is to recognize them and then have a plan to deal with them. Many of life's risks are insurable; this is a critical way to protect your long-term goals.

I will only discuss the primary types of insurance you need.

Keep in mind that insurance companies are in business to make a profit. If you have accumulated enough assets, consider the benefits of self-insuring some risks and saving the premiums.

Health Insurance

Health insurance covers medical expenses, hospitalization, and other healthcare-related costs. You may be covered under your employer's plan if you are employed.

Why you need it: Health insurance is critical coverage for everyone. Depending on the services covered by any plan and your specific medical requirements, you may need to purchase supplemental coverage.

If you are purchasing your health insurance, consider the deductible amount. A deductible is the out-of-pocket amount you pay before your insurance coverage kicks in. Plans with higher deductibles typically have lower monthly premiums. A high-deductible plan may be cost-effective if you're generally healthy and don't anticipate frequent medical expenses. A lower-deductible plan may provide better financial security if you have ongoing medical needs or a family to cover.

Life Insurance

Life insurance pays a lump sum or regular payments to beneficiaries upon the policyholder's death. See Chapter 32 for a discussion of this much-misunderstood coverage.

Why you need it: Life insurance is crucial if you have dependents, like children or a spouse who rely on your income. It can cover funeral expenses, pay off debts, and provide ongoing financial support to your family.

The amount of life insurance you need depends on your debts, ongoing expenses, the need to fund education, and how many years of income you want to replace for your beneficiaries. A common rule of thumb is that you need enough insurance to replace ten times your annual salary.

Disability Insurance

Disability insurance offers income protection if you cannot work due to a disabling injury or illness. Many larger employers offer long-term disability coverage as part of their group plans.

Why you need it: Your ability to earn an income is one of your most valuable assets. Disability insurance ensures that you continue to receive a portion of your income even if you can't work.

Disability insurance typically doesn't have deductibles. Instead, it has options for different waiting periods before you start to receive benefits. A shorter period may result in higher premiums but faster access to benefits.

Personal Liability Insurance

Liability insurance protects you from legal claims and expenses if you are found legally responsible for causing injury or property damage to others. If you own a home or have significant assets, you should consider this insurance.

Why you need it: Accidents can lead to costly lawsuits. Personal liability insurance safeguards your financial well-being by covering legal fees and potential damages awarded to the injured party.

Personal liability insurance often doesn't have deductibles. Review the policy limits to ensure sufficient coverage based on your assets and potential liability.

Long-term Care Insurance

These policies cover the cost of long-term care services, like nursing home care or in-home assistance, for individuals who cannot perform daily living activities independently.

Why you need it: By some estimates, 70% of adults aged 65 years and older will require long-term care at some point in their lives. The average length of stay in long-term care is 3.2 years.

This insurance helps cover the significant expenses associated with long-term care, ensuring you receive the support you need without depleting your savings or burdening your loved ones.

Long-term care insurance policies may offer different deductible options or elimination periods. The deductible represents the days you must pay for care out of pocket before the insurance coverage begins. Choosing the right deductible depends on your financial situation and how long you can cover care expenses independently. A more extended elimination period can lower your premiums but requires you to have sufficient savings to bridge the gap.

Buying Insurance Directly

Purchasing insurance directly from an insurance company, bypassing the agent, has pros and cons.

Pros:

- **Cost savings:** You can save on commissions or broker fees by purchasing insurance directly from the insurance company.
- **Direct communication:** Dealing directly with the insurance company lets you get information about policies, coverage, and claims directly from the source, which may result in quicker responses and resolution

of issues.
- **Choice and customization:** You can compare insurance companies and their policies when buying directly. This gives you more control over finding a policy that best suits your needs and budget.
- **No conflicts of interest:** Insurance agents or brokers might push specific policies that earn them higher commissions, even if they aren't the best fit for you. By purchasing directly from the company, you can avoid potential conflicts of interest.

Cons:

- **Limited guidance:** Without an agent or broker to assist you, you may have to navigate the complexities of insurance policies independently. This could be challenging, especially if you're unfamiliar with insurance terminology or specific coverage needs.
- **Lack of personalized advice:** An insurance agent can provide customized guidance based on your unique situation and requirements.
- **Time-consuming:** Researching and comparing policies from various insurance companies can be time-consuming.
- **Potential bias:** While agents may have conflicts of interest, they can also provide valuable insights into the reputation and reliability of different insurance companies.
- **Limited product offerings:** Some insurance companies may not offer their full range of products directly to consumers. You could miss out on specialized or bundled insurance options only available through agents or brokers.

Company Ratings

Whatever type of insurance you buy, you want to be sure the insurance company will pay your claim.

A critical part of your due diligence is your insurance company's rating. Respected independent rating agencies include AM Best, Moody's, S&P Global, and Fitch Ratings. You can find the grading system used by these agencies with an explanation of what each grade means, at TrustLayer.

Generally, if your insurer is rated from B+ to A++ they would be considered secure. You can find an insurance company's ratings on its website or the website of the rating agencies.

Rating agencies can differ in their assessment of financial strength. Consider ratings from two or more agencies before making a decision.

Ratings change. Check the ratings of your insurance company annually.

Wealthier Tip

A critical part of DIY planning is recognizing insurable risks and buying insurance that mitigates these risks.

Chapter 32
A Mind-blowing Life Insurance Secret

Simply stated, § 30.3(a) of Insurance Regulation 194 requires an insurance producer to provide in all cases a mandatory initial disclosure to a purchaser. Section 30.3(b) of Insurance Regulation 194 requires a disclosure of compensation amounts, but only if the purchaser asks for that information
—New York State Department of Financial Services, Frequently Asked Questions, Insurance Regulation 194

The laws vary by state, but in New York State (and other states) your insurance agent is required to disclose the amount of their compensation if you ask.

Few consumers ask. You should be one of them.

You should also ask whether they discount their commissions. That possibility is the "mind-blowing" secret.

Life insurance is a subject few want to confront, but it's critical to your financial planning process. If you're young, it may not seem relevant or urgent, but the whole point is to protect your loved ones in the event of an unexpected loss.

Life insurance is complex, which benefits insurance companies and agents. While most agents are professional and ethical, some aren't, which gives the industry an undeserved negative reputation. It's also dense and boring.

Don't let that stop you from confronting your need for life insurance. If anyone depends on your income, you should purchase life insurance. Any competent agent can explain which type of life insurance applies to your situation. I'm only scratching the surface here.

Term Insurance

The least expensive life insurance you can buy is term insurance. It will provide coverage for a stated period, like twenty years. Think of term insurance like renting a house. You don't build equity, but it provides shelter and comfort.

You can purchase term insurance coverage for different fixed periods of time and with premiums that are level, annually renewable, or decreasing.

If you require coverage after the fixed term, the renewal rates may be unaffordable.

If you can't afford to pay a higher premium, buy term. Whatever its limitations, having it is better than not having any insurance protection. For younger investors, term is often the best option because it's inexpensive.

If you are one of those rare investors who can buy term and invest the difference in premiums between term and whole life insurance, then term is particularly attractive (assuming you won't require life insurance protection for your entire life).

Whole Life Insurance

Unlike term policies, which protect you for a finite period, whole life insurance, commonly called permanent life insurance (PLI), is designed to provide coverage for your entire life. You pay annual premiums.

PLI policies build cash value, which is the savings component. Part of each premium payment goes toward building this cash value over time. The insurance company invests or holds these funds, and they grow tax-deferred.

You can borrow against the cash value or withdraw it, but doing so will reduce the death benefit (if not repaid) and impair the policy's investment performance.

PLI policies are a good choice for those with a permanent need for life insurance or who value the benefit of accumulating significant cash over time and can afford the higher premium.

Many types of PLI exist, but I suggest you start by focusing on blended whole life and universal life. You may be able to negotiate a discounted commission on these two types of policies.

- **Blended whole life insurance:** Combines traditional whole life insurance with term life insurance. Part of the premium pays for the whole life insurance, which has a cash value component, while the rest pays for term insurance, which is less expensive and has no cash value.
- **Universal life insurance:** A type of PLI with flexible premiums, death benefits, and a savings element that grows on a tax-deferred basis. A portion of your premium goes toward your death benefit, while the rest is invested into a savings account which can fluctuate based on interest rates.

Blended whole life may be a good choice if you want permanent coverage with cash value growth, at an affordable premium.

Universal life may be a good choice for those who need lifetime coverage, flexibility in premium payments and death benefit amounts.

How the Wealthy Buy Insurance

Many high-net-worth people don't buy insurance from their local agent. They use a small group of "fee-only" insurance consultants who negotiate commissions and structure policies that benefit their clients. These consultants don't receive commissions. They are paid hourly. Their advice is 100% objective. You can find fee-only consultants on Glenn S. Daily's website, a fee-only insurance consultant.

Scott Witt, the founder of Witt Actuarial Services, is such an advisor. In the Foreword to *Insider Trading in the Life Insurance Market*, by Chuck Hinners, Witt wrote, "One of the dirtiest little secrets of the life insurance industry is that there is an alternative to paying full commissions. Why isn't this common knowledge? Because the life insurance industry is dominated by agents that push full-commission designs and the companies that sell them."

Why Commissions Matter

Agents receive a commission of 80%–100% of the first year's premium for term insurance. First-year commissions for PLI policies average 85% of the premium. Agents earn an additional commission at each anniversary.

You may be able to negotiate commissions on a blended whole life policy to as low as 15% of premiums and on a universal life policy to as low as 3% of premiums. Few agents are willing to do this, and few insurance companies permit them to do so, but it doesn't hurt to ask.

If you use a fee-only insurance consultant, they can often get these discounts for you.

Reduced commissions can mean a policy that generates cash value quicker and accumulates more value over time.

There are circumstances under which obtaining a discounted commission on a universal life policy can make the policy competitive with term insurance when you consider the cash value of the universal life policy and the ability to fund the policy for life. Ask your insurance agent or fee-only insurance consultant to run illustrations.

An Illustration

Even with reduced commissions, the difference in premiums between a term policy and a blended whole life or universal policy may still be a barrier to many DIY investors.

A 40-year-old male can purchase a $1 million, 20-year term policy for around $600 annually. A blended whole life or universal policy premium for the same insured will be around $16,000 annually. That's a big difference, but look at what you get, assuming you are able to negotiate the agent's commission.

The term policy will expire at age 60 and have zero value, unless you have "invested the difference", in which case it could have significant value.

At age 67, the blended whole life policy will have a projected cash value of $792,957 and a guaranteed cash value of $397,216. The guaranteed cash value of this policy will continue to increase after age 67 as long as premiums are paid.

At age 67, the universal life policy will have a projected cash value of $791,849 and a guaranteed cash value of $292,959. The guaranteed cash value peaks for this policy when you reach age 73 and declines for each ensuing year.

The projected cash value estimates how much the policy will be worth based on current assumptions and market conditions. The guaranteed cash value is the minimum amount the policy will be worth, regardless of market conditions. The guaranteed cash value is typically lower than the projected cash value but provides a safety net if the market doesn't perform as expected.

Wealthier Tip

If you need insurance and are looking for the lowest premium, buy term. If you can afford a higher premium, see if a blended whole life or a universal life policy suits you, but try to find an agent who will discount commissions on those policies. If you don't need life insurance for your entire life, and have the discipline to "invest the difference", term insurance may be the optimal choice.

Chapter 33
Uninsurable Risks

> *Uninsurable risk: A risk that insurance companies cannot or do not want to insure.*
> —Julia Kagan, "Uninsurable Risk: Definition and Examples," *Investopedia*

Uninsurable risks are those that insurance companies are unwilling or unable to cover due to certain inherent characteristics. Some reasons a risk may be considered uninsurable include losses with a catastrophic potential, like those incurred due to war or terrorism.

Moral hazards are also not insurable because the insured could be incentivized to act recklessly or take undue risks because they know they are insured against the consequences (e.g., extreme sports activities, criminal acts, and self-inflicted injuries).

Listed below are common uninsurable risks that should be on your radar with suggestions for how to deal with them.

Career Risk

The rapid progression of artificial intelligence (AI) and robotics has made career risk a concern for many Americans. By some estimates, AI could replace 300 million full-time jobs, including a quarter of work tasks in the U.S. and Europe.

Planning for career risk involves taking proactive steps to enhance your employability, adaptability, and financial stability.

Strategies to help you prepare for career risk:

- **Continuous learning and skill development:** Invest in your education and skill development. Stay up-to-date with industry trends,

technology advancements, and new qualifications relevant to your field. Continuous learning can make you more valuable to employers and increase your chances of remaining employable even during economic downturns and technological disruption.
- **Networking:** Build and maintain a solid professional network. Attend industry events, conferences, and networking gatherings to connect with colleagues, mentors, and potential employers. A robust network can provide job opportunities and valuable support during career transitions.
- **Career development and growth:** Seek opportunities for career advancement within your current organization or explore new roles that align with your long-term goals.
- **Side projects and freelancing:** Consider working on side projects or freelancing to diversify your income stream.
- **Have a backup plan:** Have a contingency plan in case you lose your job. Consider alternative career paths or industries where your skills and experience could be valuable.

Longevity Risk

While the risk of outliving your savings is not directly insurable, you can manage it by planning for a long retirement and considering retirement products that provide lifetime income, like immediate and deferred annuities.

If you are a millennial, you won't need to confront the need to purchase an annuity (to deal with longevity risk) for many years, so you can skip the section on annuities. That doesn't mean you can't start dealing with longevity risk now by saving as early as possible, investing intelligently and responsibly and taking advantage of compounding.

Engaging in these activities will provide a bigger portfolio so you can mitigate the risk of outliving your money.

Annuities

You could consider an immediate or deferred annuity for a portion (no more than one-third) of your monthly expenses.

Immediate annuities: An immediate annuity is an insurance contract that provides income payments to the annuitant (the person who purchases the annuity) starting immediately after the initial payment. The annuitant makes a lump-sum payment to the insurance company or financial institution issuing the immediate annuity.

After a short period (usually within a month or a year), the insurance company begins to make regular payments to the annuitant, either for a fixed number of years or for the rest of the annuitant's life (or the life of the surviving spouse or partner), depending on the chosen payout option.

Deferred annuities: A deferred annuity is an insurance contract that provides a stream of income payments with a delay between the purchase and payout phases. The annuitant makes a lump sum or periodic premium payments into the deferred annuity over an accumulation phase, which can be several years or even decades.

After the accumulation phase, the annuitant can start receiving regular payments, either as a lump sum, a series of payments over time, or as an income stream for life.

Deferred annuities can be further categorized into fixed, variable, or indexed annuities, depending on how the funds are invested and the level of risk involved.

- If you are a conservative investor looking for a guaranteed rate of interest, you should consider a fixed annuity. You will know exactly how much you will receive once payments start flowing.
- With a variable annuity, your payment will vary depending on the performance of the investment options you choose.
- With an indexed annuity, your returns are based on the returns of a linked market index (like the S&P 500 index). You receive a level of protection against negative returns of this index and, in some cases, a guaranteed level of lifetime income. According to FINRA, "Indexed annuities are complex financial instruments, and retirement experts warn that such annuities include a number of features that may result in lower returns than an investor might expect."

Deferred annuities often have layers of fees that are not easy to uncover. When deciding on whether to purchase an annuity, you need to do an in-depth analysis of those fees and compare them to other investments.

The lower returns referenced by FINRA on indexed annuities are due to high fees.

You should also be aware that earnings withdrawn from fixed index annuities (funded with after-tax money) are taxed as ordinary income and not capital gains.

Some well-regarded annuity providers, each of which is rated A++ by AM Best, include:

- Massachusetts Mutual Life Insurance Company
- USAA Life Insurance Company
- New York Life Insurance Company
- TIAA-CREF Life Insurance Company

Divorce Risk

Consider having a prenuptial agreement in place before getting married. A "prenup" is a legally binding contract outlining how assets, debts, and other financial matters will be divided in divorce. It can provide clarity and minimize conflicts if a divorce occurs.

Raising the subject of a prenup can be awkward, but it's often in the best interest of both parties to have one. An even more delicate subject is a postnuptial agreement.

A postnuptial, "postnup", or post-marital agreement is a legally binding contract a couple enters into after marriage. A postnup outlines how the couple's assets, debts, and other financial matters will be divided in the event of divorce or separation.

As with a prenup, the parties will likely find mutually agreeing on the terms of the agreement less stressful than waiting until the marriage implodes.

Prenups and postnups are subject to state laws, which can vary. Each party to the agreement should retain a competent family law attorney to ensure the agreement complies with the current legal requirements of your jurisdiction and serves your intended purpose.

Wealthier Tip

Just because a risk isn't insurable doesn't mean you shouldn't plan for it. Thinking ahead protects your assets and helps you meet your goals.

170

Part Eight
Securing Shelter

Don't believe
what "they" tell you.

Chapter 34
Buy or Rent?

A monthly mortgage payment is often considered a forced savings account that helps homeowners build a net worth about 40 times higher than that of a renter.
—Lawrence Yun, Chief Economist, National Association of Realtors

One of the more exciting financial decisions young people make is to buy a home. From a strictly financial standpoint, there are pros and cons to both buying and renting, but even more than some other financial choices, this decision must align with your values and lifestyle.

As with so many financial questions, powerful vested interests have a huge stake in the housing market. Much of the information you're exposed to isn't objective.

According to Open Secrets, the real estate industry spent more than $135 million on lobbying in 2022, using 624 lobbyists. Their agenda is to protect the interests of their members, which means encouraging home ownership and the use of realtors to buy and sell property.

The securities industry is no slouch in the lobbying department, either (see Chapter 11). Its interest is increasing assets under management because that's usually the basis for calculating the fees of its members (see Chapter 39).

When you buy a home, that money is not available for investing.

These conflicts of interest can impact the objectivity of advice relating to home ownership.

Pros and Cons of Home Ownership

Pros:

- **Equity:** Owning a home allows you to build equity over time as you pay off your mortgage. Equity can be used for future financial endeavors or as an investment.
- **Stability and control:** Home ownership provides stability and control over your living space. You can make modifications, decorate, and manage the property according to your preferences without worrying about a landlord's restrictions.
- **Potential for appreciation:** Historically, real estate tends to appreciate over time, which means the value of your home could increase.
- **Tax benefits:** You may benefit from tax deductions on mortgage interest payments and property taxes, reducing your overall tax burden.
- **Sense of belonging:** Owning a home often fosters a stronger sense of belonging and community as you put down roots in a particular neighborhood.

Cons:

- **Financial commitment:** Buying a home typically requires a significant financial commitment, including a down payment, closing costs, and ongoing mortgage payments.
- **Maintenance and repairs:** You're responsible for maintaining your home and covering repair costs.
- **Limited flexibility:** Owning a home can limit your flexibility to move quickly if you need to relocate for work or personal reasons.
- **Property value fluctuations:** While property values can appreciate, they can also decline.
- **Higher initial costs:** Renting usually involves lower initial costs than buying a home.
- **Property taxes and insurance:** Property taxes and homeowner's insurance can add to the ongoing costs of home ownership and can increase over time.

There are additional factors to consider:

1. **Predicting future real estate prices is impossible because too many variables impact those prices, like historical trends, inflation, supply and demand dynamics, interest rates, recent market trends,**

government policies, and rental market trends. Real estate markets can also vary significantly by location.
2. Wealth advisors often contend that owning a home is a "terrible investment" because it depletes resources that could be invested in a diversified portfolio of stocks and bonds, which would yield higher expected returns over time. The problem for many is that they don't invest the difference; they spend it. Also, simply comparing investment returns doesn't account for the fact that you derive a benefit from living in a home you own. You get no additional utility from owning an **S&P 500 index fund.**

When It Makes Sense to Rent

Deciding between buying and renting a home becomes particularly challenging when you reside in an area with steep real estate prices. Renting is often a better option as the ratio of the home's purchase price to the annual rent climbs higher.

To compute this ratio, follow these steps:

1. **Multiply your monthly rent by 12 to obtain the annual rent cost.**
2. **Divide the purchase price of the home by the annual rent cost to derive the purchase price to annual rent ratio.**

Some experts believe renting is the preferable choice when the purchase price to annual rent ratio is more than 20. Fidelity has a useful "rent vs buy" calculator on its website.

Many experts also agree that you should rent unless you plan on staying in a home for at least two years and perhaps longer.

Why You Should Buy

There are several studies indicating that homeowners are more financially stable than renters, but it's not clear whether buying a home makes homeowners more financially stable, or more financially stable people can afford to buy homes.

A Survey of Consumer Finances by the Federal Reserve found that the median net worth of homeowners in the U.S. in 2019 was $255,000 compared to only $6300 for renters.

Another study by the Joint Center for Housing Studies at Harvard University found that home ownership has consistently been associated with more significant wealth accumulation among lower-income families and minorities.

Mortgages

If you decide to buy, the next critical decision is choosing between an adjustable-rate mortgage (ARM) and a fixed-rate mortgage (FRM).

ARMs offer borrowers an interest rate that can fluctuate over time. Typically, ARMs have an introductory fixed-rate period, followed by regular adjustments based on an index (which is often tied to U.S. Treasury Department security yields).

The interest rate of an ARM is lower than a comparable fixed-rate mortgage during the introductory period (typically three, five, seven, or 10 years).

FRMs are straightforward loans with a constant interest rate throughout the loan term, usually 15, 20, or 30 years.

By some estimates, roughly 80% of mortgages in the U.S. are FRMs, often with a 30-year fixed maturity, but ARMs are becoming more popular.

The U.S. is the only country in the world where fixed-rate mortgages dominate the market.

You should be aware that:

1. **During the introductory period, the interest rate of ARMs is lower than a comparable fixed-rate mortgage.**
2. **ARMs have caps limiting the amount the interest rate can increase in each adjustment period (the time the interest rate can be reset). There is also a cap on the total interest increase over the loan's life. A typical adjustment period cap is 2%. A typical lifetime cap is 5% to 6% above the initial interest rate.**

Economists believe mortgage choice is complex because it involves "uncertainty in inflation and interest rates, borrowing constraints, illiquid assets, uninsurable risk in labor income, and the need to plan over a long horizon."

Distilling these issues to help homeowners make the right choice for their unique circumstances is challenging. A few thoughts to consider:

- There's general agreement that an ARM works well for someone who plans to move or refinance before the initial adjustment period ends.
- If you are taking out a large mortgage, the lower introductory interest rate of an ARM could save you significant money.
- Some economists advocate for ARMs when the monthly cost is relatively low compared to your income and you have a stable income and a lower aversion to risk.
- There's research indicating that ARMs "tend to on average have lower interest rates than fixed-rate mortgages."
- According to the Urban Institute, concern about the risk posed by ARMs is overblown. Its research found ARMs "...are no riskier than other mortgage products and that their lower monthly payments could increase access to homeownership for more potential buyers."

Wealthier Tip

In most areas of the U.S., you will probably end up wealthier if you own a home. When financing a home, don't overlook the potential benefits of an adjustable-rate mortgage.

Chapter 35
To Prepay or Not to Prepay?

Deciding whether to pay off your mortgage early primarily comes down to whether your opportunity cost is greater than or less than your mortgage cost.
—Michael R. Roberts, Professor of Finance, The Wharton School of the University of Pennsylvania, "Should I Pay Off My Mortgage Early in This Economy?"

Deciding whether you should pay off your mortgage as part of your preretirement planning can be both an emotional and a financial issue.

There's comfort in being debt-free. Securing shelter for you and your loved ones may reduce anxiety and allow you to spend your prior mortgage payment on activities you enjoy, or to invest it with growth potential.

Financially, there are issues you need to consider before making this critical decision.

Conflicts of interest can result in information that reflects the economic interest of bankers, realtors, and the securities industry.

As you consider whether to pay off your mortgage early, focus on these issues:

- **Prioritize debt:** It makes little sense to pay off a relatively low-interest mortgage while carrying high-interest debt (like credit card debt). Prioritize paying off high-interest debt.
- **Add to retirement accounts:** Instead of paying off your mortgage, determine whether it might be more advantageous to increase contributions to your retirement plans (401[k] plans, traditional and

Roth IRAs, or other retirement accounts).
- **Refinancing:** Check to see if it's possible to refinance your mortgage with a lower interest rate and maybe a shorter term. You could also accelerate your principal payments (if there's no prepayment penalty) and pay off your mortgage more quickly.

Here's what you need to know as you dive into this decision.

Lower Expenses

Paying off your mortgage reduces your expenses. Lower fixed costs mean you may not have to dip into your portfolio as much to fund your expenses in retirement. This can be especially beneficial in a down market where you might otherwise have to sell stocks at a loss to meet your monthly nut.

Liquidity

Liquidity is the amount of money you have readily available for investment and spending. Examples of liquid assets include cash, money market accounts, and Treasury Bills. If you pay off your mortgage early, you will be reducing liquidity by the amount needed to eliminate your mortgage.

Determining the amount of liquid assets you need in retirement is essential to deciding whether to pay off your mortgage. The calculation should be conservative because many events are challenging to predict, like a healthcare crisis, job loss, or spousal death.

If paying off your mortgage impairs your ability to deal with these situations, you should reconsider your decision.

Liquidity might not be an issue if you have a hefty retirement account or other liquid assets, like bonds that pay little interest. Using some of those funds to pay down or eliminate your mortgage might make sense.

Investing

When you pay off a mortgage, those funds are no longer available for investing.

Depending on the rate you are paying for your mortgage and the expected returns from your investments, you may achieve superior earnings by investing the funds you would have used to eliminate mortgage debt.

But there's a reason returns are qualified by referring to them as "expected." The stock market doesn't always perform as predicted. Any number of factors—like geopolitical and domestic policy changes—can impact your returns positively or negatively.

Another issue is discipline. Will you really invest your prior mortgage payment, or will you spend it?

Taxes

When deciding whether to pay off your mortgage, also consider the impact of taxes.

Calculate the net cost of keeping your mortgage, which involves considering your tax bracket and whether you itemize your deductions.

When projecting the return on your investments, you should consider the impact of taxes on short-term and long-term capital gains.

Make Your Own Choice

The decision whether to pay off a mortgage is complicated, with widely divergent views. Those who espouse debt-free living oppose all debt, including a mortgage. Others advocate holding on to a large mortgage for as long as possible.

If you have a fear of the stock market, the idea of investing the funds you would use to pay off the mortgage won't appeal to you. You should still run the numbers, especially if you hold funds in a taxable account, because the historical returns of investing in the stock market may overcome your anxiety.

What about the value of the peace of mind of living in a home with no mortgage?

Michael R. Roberts, Professor of Finance at The Wharton School of the University of Pennsylvania, isn't impressed by this benefit. "If we're going to acknowledge the psychological benefit—whatever it may be—of paying down a mortgage early, we also have to acknowledge the financial cost: reduced investment earnings, loss of liquidity, and increased risk."

While there is no right or wrong answer, you might find comfort from this comment in Kiplinger: "I've yet to find someone who regrets not having a mortgage in retirement."

Wealthier Tip

Whether to pay off your mortgage early is a complex decision with major financial ramifications worthy of careful deliberation.

Part Nine
Beat Your Brain

Conquer the forces aligned against you.

Chapter 36
Will Power

Without a comprehensive estate plan, your assets will be distributed according to the intestate succession laws of your state. This may result in an unfavorable distribution of your property, with unintended beneficiaries receiving shares that you would not have chosen yourself.
—Heritage Law Office, "What Are The Potential Consequences of Not Having An Estate Plan?"

For DIY financial planners, estate planning is the most straightforward task, but finding the willpower (pun intended) to take the first step can be difficult.

By some estimates, 68% of Americans don't have any estate planning documents. Twenty-five percent die without a will. Almost 40% say they won't bother with estate planning until their life is in danger.

Like life insurance, estate planning is a way to protect and care for your loved ones, but it's hard to face the reality, especially when you're young and it feels far off.

If you are male and your partner is a woman, she will likely outlive you. Approximately 75% of women will become widows. This isn't surprising because women tend to outlive men and often marry older men. The average age of widows is only 59.

There's evidence that the inability to confront our mortality has a basis in neuroscience.

Researcher Yair Dor-Ziderman at Bar Ilan University in Israel, together with his colleagues, conducted a study on this subject and found, "The brain does not accept that death is related to us. We have this primal mechanism that means when the brain gets information that links self to death, something tells us it's not reliable, so we shouldn't believe it."

My advice: Believe it, and make a plan.

- **Plan early.** While your chances of dying prematurely between the ages of 35 and 44 are small, they aren't nonexistent. In 2020, the death rate for this age group per 100,000 of the population for men was 325.5, and for women, it was 170.7. That's why you should have a will even if you are young and don't have a significant estate.
- **Update your plan at different stages in your life.** Triggering events include marriage and partnerships, having children, asset accumulation, and planning for retirement.

The Easy Part

Estate planning for DIY financial planners could not be easier.

Start by completing (or updating) your beneficiary designations on your retirement accounts and insurance policies.

Each state has a list of formalities that must be observed for estate planning documents to be given legal effect. That's why you should retain a qualified trusts and estates attorney in your state of residence.

Some states certify attorneys in different specialties. If you live in one of those states, interview attorneys certified in wills, trusts, and estates.

Another good resource is The American College of Trust and Estate Counsel website, a national organization of more than 2,400 lawyers and law professors peer-elected to membership.

If using an attorney in your state of residence is outside your budget, there are online resources that will prepare a will for you. Before using these services, you should be aware of their limitations:

- The wills they generate may not be valid in your state of residence.
- They are unsuitable if you have complex family or estate planning issues.

- They may not have the ability to create trusts.
- They may not have attorney support to respond to questions.

The Hard Part

Finding the "willpower" to initiate the process and update it periodically can be difficult.

Perhaps it will be easier now that you understand how your brain resists confronting the reality of your inevitable death.

Wealthier Tip

Overcome your brain's resistance to confronting your mortality by implementing an estate plan to provide for your loved ones.

Chapter 37
Don't Be A Stranger

> *I don't think you have to do this weekly or monthly, but as life changes and your goals begin to change and evolve, you can reevaluate your situation and see if what you're doing still makes sense.*
> —Jordan Patrick, CFP, "I'm a Financial Advisor: Here's How Often You Should Review Your Financial Plan," *GoBankingRates*

A financial plan is like using GPS to get to a destination. You rely on the fact that the GPS is constantly updated to account for detours and other changes.

Your financial plan isn't static. It has to change when your goals or personal financial situation changes. It also has to adapt to economic and market conditions.

At a minimum, you should review your financial plan annually to ensure it remains aligned with your current situation. If your financial situation changes rapidly, you may need to review it more frequently.

Agenda for Annual Reviews

An annual review of your financial plan should include any changes in your situation, investment portfolio, tax planning, estate planning, retirement planning, and insurance coverage (especially life and disability insurance).

Here are some triggers for an update.

- **Life-altering events:** Life rarely goes the way we envision. It's filled with life-altering events, positive (financial windfall, career

advancement, new relationships) and negative (divorce, illness, loss of a loved one). Some of these events can significantly alter your financial status.
- **Economic factors:** Changes in interest rates, fluctuations in the stock market, shifts in inflation rates, changes in tax laws, and unexpected changes in the job market could trigger a review.

Outsmart Procrastination

Revisiting your financial plan should rank high on your to-do list, but chores, like going to the dentist, budgeting, and doing housework, cause us to procrastinate.

According to Joseph Ferrari, an author and expert on procrastination, about 20% of all adults are chronic procrastinators. To put this number in context, he notes, "That's higher than depression, higher than phobia, higher than panic attacks and alcoholism."

Other research suggests that 95% of us procrastinate to some degree.

If you procrastinate and fail to update your financial plan regularly, you may not reach your short- or long-term goals.

Procrastination can also lead to adverse health consequences due to higher stress and less attention to wellness.

To stop procrastinating, it helps to know the root cause of your hesitation.

Procrastination can be rooted in a fear of performing the task poorly, being disorganized, or even having attention deficit disorder. A common cause of procrastination is perfectionism. Perfectionists fear failure, making mistakes, or disapproval.

Another cause of procrastination is a lack of organization caused by the mistaken belief that we don't need to do the task at hand because we have a superior memory and don't need to memorialize important events.

Here are some tips that will help you overcome your tendency to procrastinate.

- **Reframe change as positive and necessary.** Tell yourself that

updating your financial plan is the responsible and intelligent way to reach your goals, which is important for you and your loved ones.
- **Break your financial planning review into small steps.** If it will take two hours, set aside thirty minutes daily for four days instead of tackling it in one sitting.
- **Avoid distractions.** Use a quiet space for your review. Don't disrupt your work by engaging with social media or responding to emails.
- **Here's a productivity hack:** Use two cell phones. Your "cocaine phone" is where you will put your addictive and time-consuming apps and information. Your "kale phone" is for essential apps and information. When you don't want to be distracted, keep only your "kale phone" with you.
- **Use technology.** There are apps that can help you break down larger tasks into smaller, more manageable steps and remind you when to start each. If you find yourself distracted by social media or other online distractions, software programs can block these sites during certain times of the day.
- **Use** goal-setting apps. These apps can help you set achievable goals and track your progress toward meeting them.
- **Use** mindfulness apps. They can help you reduce stress and anxiety and help you focus on the present moment.

Wealthier Tip

Commit to updating your financial plan regularly by understanding and addressing the reasons you procrastinate.

Chapter 38
Brain Barriers

FMRI studies suggest that when you imagine your future self, your brain does something weird: It stops acting as if you're thinking about yourself. Instead, it starts acting as if you're thinking about a completely different person.
—Jane McGonigal, "Our Puny Human Brains Are Terrible at Thinking About the Future," *Slate*

By now, you know what you need to do to engage in financial planning. You still may need help to implement these recommendations.

Why is that?

We're not good at planning, but it's not entirely our fault. Our brains are wired not to care about our future selves.

Temporal Discounting

What happens to our brain when we contemplate retirement planning?

The brain engages in what's known as "temporal discounting," causing us to place more value on immediate rather than future rewards. Temporal discounting impacts our daily decisions, but we often don't appreciate that our brain is programmed to work against our best interests.

- Do these examples of temporal discounting remind you of your behavior?
- Eat a high-calorie meal now instead of sticking to a healthy diet for long-term health benefits.
- Opt for a small, immediate cash reward instead of waiting for a larger payout in the future.

- Decide to skip exercise today despite knowing the long-term benefits of regular physical activity.
- Take out a loan or pay on credit instead of saving up for a purchase over time.
- Choose to procrastinate on important tasks instead of working on them and reaping the benefits later.

Protecting Your Retirement — From Yourself

UCLA researcher Hal Hershfield says, "When people think of themselves in the future, it feels to them like they are seeing a different person entirely...like a stranger on the street."

To overcome temporal discounting:

- **Make retirement feel closer.** Visualize your retired life. Writing your "retirement story" can make it feel more natural and proximate.
- **Break planning into smaller goals.** Instead of saving for one far-off goal, set nearer-term targets like maxing out your 401(k) this year. Achieving smaller goals keeps you motivated.
- **Automate savings and investments.** Set up automatic transfers from your paycheck into retirement accounts.
- **Use decision tools.** Some employers provide calculators that illustrate your estimated retirement income based on how much you're currently saving.
- **Focus on purpose and legacy.** Thinking about what you want to accomplish and the legacy you want to leave can make retirement more meaningful and worth sacrificing for today.
- **Seek accountability.** Tell others your retirement goals and have them help you stick to your savings plan. One study found that individuals had a 95% probability of completing a goal if they had "a specific accountability appointment" with someone monitoring their progress.

Wealthier Tip

Recognize temporal discounting as a barrier to planning for your future and commit to saving money for your future self.

Part Ten
Need Help?

The right advisor—
at the right price—
adds value.

Chapter 39
Decoding Fees

The industry brilliantly capitalizes on the combination of poor understanding of fees, deep loyalty, and misplaced trust.
—Larry Bates, author of *Beat the Bank*

The right advisor, at the right fee, for the right client definitely adds value to your financial planning for your long-term goals, adding expertise and wisdom that can bolster your confidence and success.

Figuring out those three "rights" is the challenge.

Registered Investment Advisors (RIAs) vs Broker-dealers

At the outset, it's important to distinguish between RIAs and broker-dealers.

RIAs are held to a "fiduciary standard." They must put the interests of their clients above their own and act with "utmost good faith."

Broker-dealers are required to recommend financial products to their clients that are in their "best interest" and to identify any potential conflicts of interest related to the sale of those products.

The exact duty broker-dealers have to their clients isn't a model of clarity. The regulation setting forth this standard is 770 pages long. However, there is wide agreement that it isn't the equivalent of the fiduciary duty to which RIAs are held.

If you want to be sure your advisor is held to a true fiduciary standard, limit your choices to RIAs.

Decoding Fees

Before you can make an intelligent decision about whether to retain the services of a financial advisor, you need to understand the fees you will incur.

How fees are presented can make it difficult to understand how much you will pay and how those fees impact your returns.

Confusion is so prevalent that many clients of broker-dealers believe they are paying nothing for their services.

Your advisor always has to get paid, as well as they should. What's vital is that you understand how they're paid and that the amount of their fees doesn't hinder your success.

Common fee structures include:

Commission-based Fees

Commission-based financial advisors (a common fee model of brokers) make money each time they buy or sell a financial product on behalf of a client. The commission is usually a percentage of the amount invested in a particular financial product, like mutual funds, stocks, or insurance products.

The commissions can be called a front-end load, charged when you initially buy an investment, or a back-end load, charged when you sell.

You may not see a direct debit from your accounts. Brokers often bundle fees into overall portfolio performance, making them less noticeable. The lack of visibility and transparency contributes to a misconception that the broker is "free" to clients.

Financial jargon and marketing tactics can also contribute to the belief that advisory services charged by brokers are free. Terms like "no upfront cost," "no out-of-pocket expenses," or "the product provider pays us" can mislead you into thinking that there are no charges for their services.

Don't believe it. Ask to see a fee schedule that sets forth all fees you will be charged.

Fee-only Advisors

Fee-only financial advisors (typically RIAs) charge a fixed fee for their services. This can be a percentage of assets under management (AUM), an hourly rate, or a flat fee for a specific service.

Assets under management (AUM): The most-common fee arrangement is a percentage of AUM—typically between 0.25% and 1.5%—of the total assets the advisor manages for you. However, hourly or retainer fees are growing in popularity.

The most straightforward argument favoring AUM fees is that the financial advisor's interests align directly with yours. If the value of your portfolio grows, the fee (as a percentage) remains the same or declines, meaning the advisor earns more in absolute terms.

Advisors who charge an AUM-based fee still have conflicts of interest. Because of increased fee potential, the advisor may be incentivized to take more than the necessary risk with your portfolio. An AUM-based advisor may also be less likely to advise you to take steps that might reduce your AUM, like paying off a mortgage, buying cash value life insurance, or purchasing a deferred annuity.

Ethical advisors—and most are ethical in my experience—will resolve these conflicts in your favor, which they are legally required to do.

An AUM-based fee may be justified by the work required to do a comprehensive financial plan, which is usually included in the services offered for no additional fee.

If you want to run your own calculation on how an AUM-based fee impacts your returns, investor advocate Larry Bates provides a very helpful calculator on his website.

Hourly rate: In the hourly-rate model, you're billed for each hour the advisor works on your financial plan or other services. Rates vary based on the advisor's experience, location, and specialization.

You only pay for the time the advisor spends on your specific needs, which is beneficial if you only need to resolve a particular issue. Hourly planners are also a resource for long-term guidance, permitting you to obtain whatever advice you need, whenever you need it, without a fixed cost.

Flat fees: The flat-fee model is a straightforward approach where the advisor charges a fixed fee for a specified package of services ranging from creating a comprehensive financial plan to ongoing portfolio management. The flat fee could be a one-time charge for a financial plan or an annual fee for ongoing services.

It has the benefit of predictability since the advisor gets paid the same amount regardless of the financial products they recommend or the time they spend.

Performance-based fee: With the performance-based model, the advisor gets paid only when your investments perform well. This model is primarily used by hedge funds.

Theoretically, it motivates the advisor to work hard to achieve positive returns but may encourage the advisor to take excessive risks in an effort to achieve higher returns (and earn higher fees).

Minimum fee: Many advisors have a minimum fee requirement. On average, it's $5,000 annually for ongoing services, which can also be expressed as a minimum amount of required assets. A typical minimum range of assets is $250,000–$1,000,000.

Wealthier Tip

Limit your choice of advisor to registered investment advisors. Understand the pros and cons of different fee arrangements.

Chapter 40
Cutting Costs

The amount you pay has a direct impact on your returns.
—Vanguard, "Smart Investment Strategies"

Like any other fees, the fees charged by financial advisors reduce your returns.

It's vital that you know what you're paying and that what you're getting is worthwhile.

If you are a DIY investor with limited assets and basic financial planning needs who requires assistance, seeking lower-cost financial advice may be prudent.

Here are some options:

Robo-advisors

Robo-advisors are platforms that use algorithms to provide investment advice and manage your portfolio. They have surged in popularity due to their relatively low fees and ease of use.

With minimal human intervention, robo-advisors are typically less expensive than traditional financial advisors. However, the lack of human support (unless you meet the minimums of some robo-advisors) means the services you will receive are limited or non-existent, especially in the area of behavioral coaching.

Leading, cost-effective robo-advisors and associated fees:

ROBO-ADVISOR	ANNUAL FEES
Betterment	0.25%–0.40%
Wealthfront	0.25%
Vanguard Digital Advisor	0.15%
Schwab Intelligent Portfolios	No advisory fees and no commissions
Fidelity GO	0.50% with a minimum $50,000 investment

Reduced-fee Financial Advisors

If you need a human advisor but are concerned about fees, lower-cost options exist to provide you with qualified advisors at a reasonable fee.

ADVISORS	ANNUAL FEES
Vanguard Personal Advisors	0.30% for accounts under $5 million
Schwab Intelligent Portfolios Premium	$300 plus $30/month
Fidelity GO	0.50%

With both Vanguard and Schwab, most advisors are Certified Financial Planners®. In all three platforms, advisors have a fiduciary relationship with their clients.

Vanguard and Schwab provide goals-based financial planning in addition to portfolio management. Fidelity offers unlimited 30-minute phone calls with a financial coach once your account reaches $25,000. Schwab has a minimum asset requirement of $25,000. Vanguard has a minimum asset requirement of $50,000.

All three are large, reputable fund families with substantial resources and impressive infrastructure.

Discount Financial Advisors

Here are some resources for finding fee-only financial planners who may be suitable for your needs and more cost-effective than a full-fee AUM-based advisor:

- **Garrett Planning Network:** The Garret Planning Network is a national network of hundreds of hourly-based financial planners who don't require any asset minimums.

- **XY Planning Network:** This is a network of Certified Financial Planners®/advisors that have no minimums.
- **NAPFA:** A leading association of fee-only financial advisors.

Some small advisory firms and family planners charge lower fees, usually based on an hourly rate. Some have no minimum number of hours you need to purchase. You can find them by doing an online search for "low-cost financial advisors" or "discount financial advisors."

Wealthier Tip

For many DIY investors who need assistance, robo-advisors and low-cost financial advisors are worthy of consideration.

Chapter 41
Studies that Quantify Value

> *Ultimately, the point isn't that advisors shouldn't follow the studies on the use and benefits of financial planning but simply that it's still necessary to apply a healthy degree of skepticism when reviewing and applying research.*
> —Derek Tharp, "Can We Trust Research On The Use And Benefits Of Financial Advisors?" *Kitces*

The studies listed below, all done by large, reputable firms, quantify the value of financial advisors. It's helpful to be familiar with them so you understand the potential benefits of using a financial advisor.

The Russell Investments Study

Russell Investments' most recent study in 2023 found that advisors confer benefits through:

- Active rebalancing
- Behavioral coaching
- Customized experience
- Tax-smart planning and investing

The Russell study doesn't provide a total value for the four critical elements of the "Value of an Advisor" formula. However, it emphasizes that these elements work together to provide a comprehensive and personalized approach to financial planning that can help investors achieve their financial goals.

In their 2022 study, Russell found these benefits might be worth as much as 4.91% of additional investment return, broken down as follows:

Active Rebalancing:	0.11%
Behavioral Coaching:	2.37%
Customized Experience:	1.21%
Tax Smart Planning and Investing:	1.22%

Note that almost half the value is attributed to behavioral coaching, which aims to help investors make rational and informed decisions with their investments and avoid impulsive ones.

The Vanguard Study

A July 2022 study by Vanguard concludes that advisors who follow Vanguard's "Advisor's Alpha framework" can add up to, or even exceed, 3% in net returns. Vanguard notes, "We do not believe this potential 3% improvement can be expected annually; rather, it is likely to be very irregular."

Here's the breakdown:

Selecting investments with	
Selecting low expense ratio funds	0.30%
Rebalancing	0.14%
Behavioral coaching	0%>2.00%
Asset location	0%–0.60%
Spending strategy (withdrawal order)	0%–1.20%

Vanguard concedes that these results will "vary significantly" depending on your circumstances.

The Morningstar Study

Morningstar published an August 28, 2013 study on the value of a financial advisor.

It used a Monte Carlo simulation and estimated that a retiree could expect to earn the equivalent of an annual return increase of 1.59%.

Caveats

While the studies quantify the value of an advisor differently, they agree that using a financial advisor can significantly enhance returns.

Derek Tharp, Ph.D., noted in his article, "Can We Trust Research On The Use and Benefits Of Financial Advisors?" that there's reason to be skeptical of studies attempting to quantify a financial advisor's value because:

1. It's "very difficult" to measure the value of a given strategy.
2. We don't know what would have happened without the advisor's advice, so we can't determine if that advice improved the outcome for a given investor. For example, if you follow the information in Chapter I about the benefit of low management fee investments, you wouldn't benefit from having an advisor suggest that strategy.
3. There's an inherent bias toward publishing studies with favorable results and not publishing those without statistically significant benefits. A study might find little or no benefit in using an advisor but would likely "just remain unpublished in the file drawers of academics."

Nevertheless, there are additional benefits to using a financial advisor that can't be quantified but shouldn't be ignored.

Opportunity cost: When you outsource financial matters to an advisor, you gain an "opportunity cost" benefit by freeing up time and resources, allowing you to focus on other important areas of your life or business. Reallocating your time can lead to increased productivity, improved decision-making, and a better overall quality of life.

Peace of mind: Outsourcing financial matters to a financial advisor can provide peace of mind by ensuring your finances are in capable hands. The value of this benefit can be measured by the reduction of stress and anxiety related to financial management and the potential increase in financial returns due to expert guidance.

Wealthier Tip

Qualified advisors can add significant tangible and intangible benefits to your present and future financial success.

Chapter 42
AI is Your New BFF

What we're trying to do is meet people where they are and allow them to ask questions in their own words, which the program can use to match them up with the best advice and ways forward.
—Nhung Ho, "AI Could Make Financial Planning More Accessible, Suggest Some in the Sector," *Investment Executive*

There's little doubt about the seismic impact artificial intelligence will have on financial planning. Many believe it will drive greater efficiencies and provide more sophisticated analytical capabilities and personalization.

Most writing about artificial intelligence focuses on how financial advisors can use AI to augment their service to investors.

But what about its impact on DIY investors?

Budgeting and Expense Tracking

AI-driven personal finance apps like PocketGuard categorize, track, and analyze your expenses, providing valuable insights into your spending habits. They can predict if you're likely to exceed your budget and even suggest changes you can make to stay on track.

Some AI applications, like Cleo, offer real-time alerts based on unusual spending activities or upcoming bills. You can chat with the app, asking questions like: "Can I afford a pizza?" and "Where can I cut back this month?"

Credit Score Monitoring

Credit Karma and Experian offer AI-powered services that track and suggest specific steps to improve your credit score.

Credit Sesame uses AI to show how future financial decisions could impact your credit score, enabling you to make informed choices. It analyzes your data and provides personalized tips for improving your credit.

Tax Planning

Intuit TurboTax and H&R Block use AI to suggest tax-saving strategies, making navigating the complex tax landscape easier. H&R Block uses machine learning models "trained with millions of tax returns, AI algorithms, and technology."

Organizing Receipts

Getting documents organized for tax preparation is a yearly nightmare for many. With Shoeboxed, you can automate this process. Use the mobile app or prepaid envelopes to scan and upload receipts, business cards, and other documents. The data is extracted and made viewable in your online Shoeboxed account.

Insurance

Insurify uses AI algorithms to provide users with personalized insurance quotes and recommendations. The platform analyzes customer information, driving records, and insurance needs to match individuals with optimal policies.

Investment Apps

Some helpful resources if you need assistance with your portfolio:

- **Portfolio Visualizer** is a powerful tool DIY investors can use to rebalance their portfolio to target allocations, compare portfolio performance to benchmarks, find optimal asset allocations, and test how a portfolio would have performed historically.
- **Stockal** can analyze your portfolio and identify areas that require rebalancing. Its rebalancing recommendations take into account your investment goals, risk tolerance, and market conditions.
- **CoinTracker** primarily serves cryptocurrency investors but offers

robust tax loss harvesting features equally valuable for traditional assets. The app can sync with various exchanges and wallets to automate the tracking and identification of tax loss harvesting opportunities. You can import investment transactions, track your cost basis, and generate tax reports with information relevant to harvesting tax loss. It provides features to help you identify and execute tax-efficient strategies for minimizing your capital gains tax liability.

Financial Planning

There are many software options for DIY financial planners. Here are some of the leading ones:

- **Empower** (formerly Personal Capital) offers a free version that includes basic financial planning features.
- **WealthTrace** permits you to make financial projections and monitor your investment holdings, performance, transactions and fees.
- **Quicken** lets you track and categorize your spending, customize a spending plan, project cash flow and track progress towards reaching your savings goals.

Behavioral Coaching

- **Streaks** is an app that helps you form good habits. It's not explicitly geared for investing but could be a valuable tool to assist with behavioral coaching. You could input positive behavior like "Don't check my portfolio for six months" or "Make monthly deposits to my portfolio."
- **ChatGPT** can serve as a primary behavioral coach, offering tips on investment psychology, answering queries, and helping you to stay disciplined. It can also answer questions about investing and financial planning.

I asked ChatGPT 4.0 five questions. The questions and ChatGPT's answers are listed below (lightly edited). These responses provided advice that is generally sound, but that's not always true with AI-generated content, so you should independently verify its output.

Q: How should I start investing?

A: Start by setting clear financial goals, understanding risk tolerance, and diversifying your investments. Don't put all your eggs in one basket.

Q: How much should I save for retirement?

A: It varies, but a common rule of thumb is to aim to save 10–15 percent of your annual income. Use a retirement calculator to tailor this estimate to your situation.

Q: How can I minimize taxes on my investments?

A: Consider tax-efficient investment vehicles like Roth IRAs or 401(k)s, and be mindful of the tax implications when buying and selling investments.

Q: Should I pay off debt or invest?

A: It depends on the interest rates. If your debt has a higher interest rate than what you'd earn through investing, focus on paying off the debt first.

Q: How do I know if I should retain a financial advisor?

A: Deciding if you need a financial advisor involves assessing your financial goals, the complexity of assets, and comfort with managing finances. If you're seeking expert guidance, peace of mind, or face intricate financial decisions, consider professional help.

Wealthier Tip

Artificial intelligence is a rapidly expanding source of valuable information for DIY investors.

Conclusion:
Trust Yourself

The Stoics know where they are going. They trust themselves and their sense of the path.
—Daily Stoic, "Trust Yourself"

You can do this.

Remember the basic guidelines:

1. **Tune out the noise of financial media.**
2. **Buy two exchange-traded funds (ETFs).**
3. **Overcome your brain's barriers to planning for the future.**
4. **Review your financial plan every year or when you have a life change.**
5. **Embrace a simple, satisfying lifestyle and live below your means.**

If retirement feels far off, that means time is on your side and now is the time to take steps toward the future you want.

The information I've offered in this book is a jumping-off point to help you own your decisions, research the right path for you, invest with confidence, and reap the rewards.

All that's left is for you to take the reins and start your path to a "wealthier" future.

Endnotes

Introduction: A Friend in Need

The introductory quote can be found at: https://www.morningstar.com/views/blog/client-engagement/what-is-financial-empowerment.

The New York Times review of *Smartest Investment*: https://www.nytimes.com/2006/10/08/business/mutfund/a-bold-insistence-on-one-way-to-invest.html?searchResultPosition=1

Derek Sivers' list of recommended books: https://www.readthistwice.com/person/derek-sivers

Kiplinger's list of classic investment books: https://www.kiplinger.com/article/investing/t031-c000-s002-boost-your-iq-with-a-good-book.html

Style Rave's must-read financial books: https://www.stylerave.com/best-must-read-financial-books/

About my on-air dispute with Jim Cramer: https://www.huffpost.com/entry/the-solin-cramer-smackdow_b_188535

Shift to index fund investing: https://www.cnbc.com/2024/01/18/passive-investing-rules-wall-street-now-topping-actively-managed-assets-in-stock-bond-and-other-funds.html#:~:text=Passive%20investment%20products%20have%20long,than%20their%20actively%20managed%20counterparts.

How millennials react to stock market volatility: https://www.ey.com/en_gl/wealth-asset-management/global-wealth-research-millennial-trends

Survey that discusses how millennials hold too much of their investments in cash: https://mybrand.schroders.com/m/425d7a1eb513d673/original/Schroders_2023_US_Retirement_Survey_Readiness_Rpt_FINAL.pdf

The allure of actively managed funds for millennials: https://www.ey.com/en_gl/wealth-asset-management/global-wealth-research-millennial-trends

The appeal of alternative investments to millennials: https://www.ey.com/en_gl/wealth-asset-management/global-wealth-research-millennial-trends

Retirement goals for millennials: https://www.bankrate.com/investing/millennials-investing-trends-and-stats/

The attitude of millennials toward traditional financial advisors: https://money.usnews.com/financial-advisors/articles/are-millennials-rejecting-financial-advisors#:~:text=It'd%20be%20more%20accurate,by%20millennials%2C%22%20he%20says

Chapter 1: Investing is Simple and Easy

The chapter quote is extracted from the book *If You Can* authored by William J. Bernstein.

Quote from Warren Buffett: https://quotefancy.com/quote/931531/Warren-Buffett-Investing-is-simple-but-not-easy

Quote from John Bogle: https://www.nytimes.com/2019/01/17/business/mutfund/john-bogle-vanguard-investment-advice.html#:~:text=%E2%80%9CIn%20investing%2C%20you%20get%20what,can%20consistently%20outsmart%20the%20market.%E2%80%9D

A list of peer-reviewed articles supporting Bogle's views on the Index Fund Advisors' website: https://www.ifa.com/academic-papers

The history of U.S. debt: https://www.theatlantic.com/business/archive/2012/11/the-long-story-of-us-debt-from-1790-to-2011-in-1-little-chart/265185/

The representative quotes:

Buffett quote: https://www.etmoney.com/learn/personal-finance/9-lessons-in-investing-by-warren-buffett/

Lynch quote: https://www.azquotes.com/quote/1259336

Malkiel quote: https://www.quotemaster.org/qbdecdfbeea12088700492644075e0658

Lewis quote: https://quotefancy.com/quote/1296513/Michael-Lewis-Wall-Street-with-its-army-of-brokers-analysts-and-advisers-funneling

The survey of economists can be found at: https://www.fraserinstitute.org/blogs/economists-unanimous-index-funds-are-investing-101#:~:text=Actually%2C%20not%20all%20economists%20say,he's%20very%20sure%20of%20it

Historical annual returns of the the FTSE Global All Cap index: research.ftserussell.com

Information about VT: https://investor.vanguard.com/investment-products/etfs/profile/vt#performance-fees

Historical annual returns of the ICE Bofa Merrill Lynch 1-3 Year US Treasury index: https://curvo.eu/backtest/en/market-index/ice-us-treasury-1-3-year-bond?currency=eur

Information about SHY: https://www.ishares.com/us/products/239452/SHY?cid=ppc:ishares_us:google:fund-names-priorities&gclid=CjwKCAjwhdWkBhBZEiwAlibLmIMefcHtZTo98kOcZ6Lc8ZpLwKfAVGyr-OWfaf-AFbyOVvxGON-6T5hoCqcYQAvD_BwE&gclsrc=aw.ds

There are many alternatives to SHY, including the Schwab Short-Term U.S. Treasury ETF (SCHO). It tracks the total return of an index that measures the performance of the short-term U.S. Treasury bond market. Its inception date was August 5, 2010. It has a low expense ratio of 0.030%. As of January 29, 2024, it had more than $12 billion under management.

Information about SCHO: https://www.schwabassetmanagement.com/products/scho.

Arguments against foreign bond diversification: https://retirementresearcher.com/need-diversify-bonds/

Vanguard's views on foreign bond diversification: https://investor.vanguard.com/investor-resources-education/understanding-investment-types/why-invest-internationally#:~:text=In%20general%2C%20Vanguard%20recommends%20that,bond%20allocation%20in%20international%20bonds

Information about IGOV: https://www.ishares.com/us/products/239830/

Historical returns of stocks and bonds: https://www.ishares.com/us/products/239830/

The difference between risk and volatility: https://www.morningstar.co.uk/uk/news/227398/whats-the-difference-between-risk-and-volatility.aspx

Vanguard's asset allocation calculator: https://investor.vanguard.com/tools-calculators/investor-questionnaire#modal-start-quiz

iPers asset allocation calculator: https://ipers.org/members/calculators/asset

Similarities and differences between index mutual funds and ETFs: https://www.forbes.com/advisor/investing/etf-vs-index-fund/#:~:text=One%20of%20the%20most%20significant,day%2C%20after%20the%20markets%20close.

Academic papers supporting Bogle's views can be found on the Index Fund Advisors' website: https://www.ifa.com/academic-papers.

Chapter 2: The Factor Factor

The chapter quote can be found at: https://www.kitces.com/blog/review-fact-fiction-factor-investing-aghassi-asness-fattouche-moskowitz-swedroe-persistence-timing/.

Information about the Goldman Sachs ActiveBeta U.S. Large Cap Equity ETF (GSLC): https://www.gsam.com/content/gsam/us/en/individual/products/etf-fund-finder/goldman-sachs-activebeta-u-s--large-cap-equity-etf.html#activeTab=overview

Dimensional Fund Advisors has been a leading fund family in the factor-based space for many years. Here's a list of its mutual funds and ETFs:

https://www.dimensional.com/us-en/funds

Chapter 3: Retirement Plan Investing

The chapter quote can be found at: https://americasbest401k.com/401k-study/.

The Morningstar quote can be found at: https://www.morningstar.co.uk/uk/news/149421/how-fund-fees-are-the-best-predictor-of-returns.aspx.

Study on the impact of high fees in retirement plans: https://www.demos.org/research/retirement-savings-drain-hidden-excessive-costs-401ks

Expense ratios for mutual funds in plans offered by the largest platforms: chrome-extension://mhnlakgilnojmhinhkckjpncpbhabphi/pages/pdf/web/viewer.html?file=https%3A%2F%2Famericasbest401k.com%2Fwp-content%2Fuploads%2F2017%2F12%2FABk_SmallBizFees_FINAL.pdf

Study on poor investment choices in small business retirement plans: https://americasbest401k.com/wp-content/uploads/2017/12/ABk_SmallBizFees_FINAL.pdf

Information about traditional IRAs: https://www.schwab.com/ira/traditional-ira

Information about Roth IRAs: https://www.schwab.com/ira/roth-vs-traditional-ira

Information about Solo 401(k)s: https://www.nerdwallet.com/article/investing/what-is-a-solo-401k

Information about SEP IRAs: https://www.irs.gov/retirement-plans/retirement-plans-faqs-regarding-simple-ira-plans#:~:text=A%20SIMPLE%20IRA%20plan%20provides,either%20matching%20or%20nonelective%20contributions.

Information about HSAs: https://www.healthcare.gov/glossary/health-savings-account-hsa/

Chapter 4: Socially Responsible Investing

The chapter quote can be found at: https://fortune.com/recommends/investing/what-is-esg-investing/.

Survey showing the interest of millennials in ESG investments: https://www.nasdaq.com/articles/how-millennials-and-gen-z-are-driving-growth-behind-esg

General information about socially responsible investing: https://www.investopedia.com/terms/s/sri.asp

Information about the number of ESG funds available to investors: https://www.nasdaq.com/articles/how-millennials-and-gen-z-are-driving-growth-behind-esg

The issue of greenwashing: https://www.nasdaq.com/articles/how-millennials-and-gen-z-are-driving-growth-behind-esg

The SEC's new rule cracking down on greenwashing: https://www.sec.gov/files/rules/final/2023/33-11238.pdf

The quote attributed to Jon Hale can be found at: https://www.nerdwallet.com/article/investing/best-esg-funds.

SEC Bulletin for investors on ESG funds: https://www.investor.gov/introduction-investing/general-resources/news-alerts/alerts-bulletins/investor-bulletins-1

Information about the S&P 500 ESG index: https://www.spglobal.com/spdji/en/indices/esg/sp-500-esg-index/#overview

Factors that contribute to lower expected returns of ESG stocks: https://papers.ssrn.com/sol3/papers.cfm?abstract_id=3498354

Stanford University survey about the willingness of millennials to sacrifice returns for the greater good: https://www.gsb.stanford.edu/sites/default/files/publication/pdfs/cgri-closer-look-98-esg-investing.pdf

Information about Vanguard's ESG U.S. Stock ETF: https://investor.vanguard.com/investment-products/etfs/profile/esgv

Information about iShares ESG Aware MSCI USA ETF: https://www.ishares.com/us/literature/fact-sheet/esgu-ishares-esg-aware-msci-usa-etf-fund-fact-sheet-en-us.pdf

Information about Vanguard's ESG International Stock ETF: https://investor.vanguard.com/investment-products/etfs/profile/vsgx

Chapter 5: Alternative Investments

The chapter quote can be found at: https://www.evidenceinvestor.com/alternative-investments-have-been-useless-since-2007/.

Views of Goldman Sachs advocating for alternatives: https://www.gsam.com/content/gsam/us/en/institutions/market-insights/gsam-insights/2023/allocating-to-alternatives.html

Average allocation of high net worth investors to alternatives: https://www.gsam.com/content/gsam/us/en/institutions/market-insights/gsam-insights/2023/allocating-to-alternatives.html

The disappointing returns of alternative investments: https://www.evidenceinvestor.com/alternative-investments-have-been-useless-since-2007/

Information about NFTs: https://www.nytimes.com/interactive/2022/03/18/technology/nft-guide.html

Pros and cons of NFTs: https://cryptonews.com/news/pros-cons-of-nfts-everything-you-need-know.htm

Size of the fractional market for art: https://www.masterworks.com/?utm_source=google+brand&utm_medium=platform&utm_campaign=Brand_Masterworks&utm_content=masterworks&gad=1&gclid=CjwKCAiA6byqBhAWEiwAnGCA416Pw6OuA2Ix1ODC-yUIInHwHpcIvgzDzUXqG-J3413P7_JuNCihTdBoCDmoQAvD_BwE&utm_flag=original-mode

The quote attributed to Mariana Custodio website: https://marianacustodio.com/the-5-biggest-art-frauds-in-contemporary-art-history/.

Risks of investing in art and collectibles: https://www.investopedia.com/articles/personal-finance/061815/risks-investing-art-and-collectibles.asp#:~:text=They%20are%20more%20difficult%20to,of%20destruction%20of%20the%20assets.

Size of the fractional market for real estate: https://fundrise.com/acq-plus/start?gclsrc=aw.ds&utm_source=google&utm_medium=cpc&utm_campaign=brand-849327244-47015505727-g&utm_content=435576490559-fundrise-e-c&gad_source=1&gclid=Cj0KCQiAuqKqBhDxARIsAFZELmJQss3IgmDeB-5drIhB424qFvrvelq6Uamed-QmNUT8_LkvWHTzCSHMaAs3VEALw_wcB

Pros and cons of investing in real estate: https://readwrite.com/real-estate-investing/

Fractional shares of stocks: https://robinhood.com/us/en/support/articles/fractional-shares/

Robinhood financial results for Q2 2023: https://investors.robinhood.com/news/news-details/2023/Robinhood-Reports-Second-Quarter-2023-Results/default.aspx

MusicSplit and ArtSplit: https://www.artsplit.com/musicsplit

Songvest: https://www.songvest.com/?utm_source=SongVest&utm_medium=GoogleSearch&utm_campaign=LeadGen&gad_source=1&gclid=Cj0KCQiAuqKqBhDxARIsAFZELmlp9nZnUoZTnNZSyvZuTBsoOnSTpMA4IWNaQQhzH-JpoS-jpH7CFb4aAgr8EALw_wcB

Royalty Exchange: https://www.royaltyexchange.com/instant-offer?ads_cmpid=1011106690&ads_adid=49202678785&ads_matchtype=b&ads_network=g&ads_creative=530521216211&utm_term=%2Broyalty%20%2Bexchange&ads_targetid=kwd-394969080372&utm_campaign=&utm_source=adwords&utm_medium=ppc&ttv=2&gad_source=1&gclid=Cj0KCQiAuqKqBhDxARIsAFZELmLthrWtFfOq5W00ykwiPMLQQ0G1w3PoCxK23w3yN-OEI_DSWW-6kVUaArt2EALw_wcB

Publica: https://publica.com/

Chapter 6: Lotto Luck

The chapter quote can be found at: https://finance.yahoo.com/news/swedroe-avoid-lotterylike-investments-100030033.html.

Lottery odds: https://www.davidson.edu/news/2023/07/19/magic-numbers-how-tilt-odds-winning-lottery-or-powerball-jackpot-your-favor#:~:text=But%20actually%20bringing%20home%20the,(slightly)%20in%20your%20favor

Paper on the role of the brain in financial decisions: https://www.redalyc.org/journal/5117/511766757004/html/#:~:text=Moreover%2C%20the%20effects%20of%20hormones,prevention%20of%20negative%20financial%20scenarios

The dopamine portfolio vs. the serotonin portfolio: https://financialpost.com/investing/investing-pro/the-dopamine-portfolio-vs-the-serotonin-portfolio-do-you-know-which-one-you-have

Loss aversion: https://thedecisionlab.com/biases/loss-aversion

Chapter 7: Cryptocurrency Confusion

The chapter quote can be found at: https://www.investors.com/news/warren-buffett-bashes-bitcoin-as-gambling-token-bitcoin-price-hovers-near-30000/.

General discussion of cryptocurrency: https://www.nerdwallet.com/article/investing/cryptocurrency

Pros and cons of investing in cryptocurrency: https://www.forbes.com/advisor/in/investing/cryptocurrency/advantages-of-cryptocurrency/

Information on the limited supply of cryptocurrency: https://www.blockchain-council.org/cryptocurrency/how-many-bitcoins-are-left/#:~:text=The%20maximum%20supply%20of%202021,the%20process%20of%20Bitcoin%20mining

Discussion of the FTX Exchange: https://www.investopedia.com/ftx-exchange-5200842

Regarding the conviction of Sam Bankman-Fried: https://www.cnbc.com/2023/11/02/sam-bankman-fried-found-guilty-on-all-seven-criminal-fraud-counts.html

Charges filed by the SEC against Binance: https://www.sec.gov/news/press-release/2023-101

The guilty plea of Changpeng Zhao and Binance's agreement to pay $4 billion: https://finance.yahoo.com/news/crypto-chief-pleads-guilty-money-230648934.html

The environmental impact of cryptocurrency mining: https://earthjustice.org/feature/cryptocurrency-mining-environmental-impacts#:~:text=Top%20down%20estimates%20of%20the,in%20the%20U.S.%20in%202021 and https://www.climate.gov/news-features/understanding-climate/climate-change-atmospheric-carbon-dioxide#:~:text=Without%20carbon%20dioxide%2C%20Earth's%20natural,causing%20global%20temperature%20to%20rise

Schwab's view of investing in cryptocurrencies: https://www.schwab.com/learn/story/are-cryptocurrency-investments-right-you#:~:text=Bitcoin%20and%20other%20cryptocurrencies%20are,their%20volatility%E2%80%94not%20intrinsic%20value

Chapter 8: Investing Myths

The chapter quote is extracted from *Winning the Loser's Game: Timeless Strategies for Successful Investing*, by Charles D. Ellis.

The risks of excessive margin trading: https://insights.som.yale.edu/insights/study-margin-trading-causes-stock-prices-to-drop-in-concert

The risks of day trading: https://www.sciencedirect.com/science/article/abs/pii/S1386418113000190

The performance of gold: https://www.statista.com/statistics/1061434/gold-other-assets-average-annual-returns-global/#:~:text=Average%20annual%20return%20of%20gold%20and%20other%20assets%20worldwide%201971%2D2022&text=Between%20January%201971%20and%20December,in%202022%20was%200.4%20percent

The dismal track record of actively managed funds: https://www.spglobal.com/spdji/en/spiva/article/spiva-us/

The track record of technical analysis: https://jonathankinlay.com/2023/01/why-technical-analysis-doesnt-work/

The expected returns of high-quality stocks: https://bookdown.org/adam_aiken/advinv/factors.html

The study showing only 4% of stocks explain the net gain for the entire U.S. stock market: https://papers.ssrn.com/sol3/papers.cfm?abstract_id=2900447

The efficiency of the stock market: https://www.investopedia.com/terms/p/price-efficiency.asp#:~:text=Price%20efficiency%20is%20the%20belief,is%20in%20the%20public%20domain

The relationship of past performance to future returns: https://insights.som.yale.edu/insights/does-mutual-fund-s-past-performance-predict-its-future

Extracts from books authored by Suze Orman and Dave Ramsey: https://www.nytimes.com/2019/10/11/business/suze-orman-robert-kiyosaki-dave-ramsey-books.html

Quote from Fidelity investments: https://www.fidelity.com/viewpoints/retirement/how-long-will-savings-last#:~:text=We%20did%20the%20math%E2%80%94looking,the%20first%20year%20of%20retirement%2C

Article by James Choi: https://papers.ssrn.com/sol3/papers.cfm?abstract_id=4203061

Chapter 9: Terrible Consequences

The chapter quote can be found at: https://papers.ssrn.com/sol3/papers.cfm?abstract_id=3213334.

Article from Retirement Researcher: https://retirementresearcher.com/occams-ignore-the-financial-media/

Tragic story of Alex Kearns: https://www.cnbc.com/2020/06/18/young-trader-dies-by-suicide-after-thinking-he-racked-up-big-losses-on-robinhood.html

Study correlating suicide rates to declines in stock market returns: https://papers.ssrn.com/sol3/papers.cfm?abstract_id=3213334

Chapter 10: Something Needs to Change

The chapter quote can be found at: https://www.bankrate.com/banking/savings/emergency-savings-report/.

Sad state of retirement savings of American workers: https://www.ebri.org/docs/default-source/rcs/rcs_22-fs-3_prep.pdf?sfvrsn=e5c83b2f_4

Inability of Americans to come up with emergency savings: https://www.bankrate.com/banking/savings/emergency-savings-report/

Savings challenges confronting millennials: https://www.napa-net.org/news-info/daily-news/what-are-401k-participation-and-savings-rates-generation#:~:text=They%20began%20saving%20at%20age,(median)%20in%20emergency%20savings

Student loan debt of millennials: https://crr.bc.edu/wp-content/uploads/2021/02/IB_21_3-1.pdf

Millennials behind older investors in retirement readiness: https://www.cnbc.com/select/millennials-behind-other-generations-retirement-savings/

Overreliance of Americans on Social Security: https://www.ssa.gov/news/press/factsheets/basicfact-alt.pdf

Projected healthcare costs for retirees: https://www.fidelity.com/viewpoints/personal-finance/plan-for-rising-health-care-costs

Credit card balances in the U.S.: https://www.newyorkfed.org/newsevents/news/research/2023/20230808

Financial struggles of older Americans: https://www.cbsnews.com/news/social-security-medicare-seniors-more-americans-struggling-to-pay-bills/

Chapter 11: A Rigged System

The chapter quote can be found at: https://hbr.org/2014/06/the-price-of-wall-streets-power.

The long-term performance of the stock market: https://www.officialdata.org/us/stocks/s-p-500/1928?amount=100&endYear=2022

Inflation concerns: https://www.forbes.com/advisor/investing/how-to-hedge-against-inflation/

Number of registered representatives in the U.S.: https://www.finra.org/media-center/statistics#key-industry-statistics

Gross revenues of broker-dealers: https://www.sifma.org/resources/research/fact-book/

Issues with self-regulation: https://scholars.law.unlv.edu/cgi/viewcontent.cgi?article=2141&context=facpub

FINRA's responsibilities: https://www.finra.org/about/what-we-do

The quote attributed to Benjamin P. Edwards: https://scholars.law.unlv.edu/cgi/viewcontent.cgi?article=2141&context=facpub.

Anti-investor lobbying efforts of the securities industry: https://www.citizen.org/article/hypnotized-by-wall-street/

Issues with mandatory arbitration: https://www.nytimes.com/2016/06/04/business/dealbook/finra-arbitration-case-offers-a-peek-into-a-murky-world.html and https://www.nber.org/system/files/working_papers/w25150/revisions/w25150.rev1.pdf

Statistics showing the lack of diversity of FINRA arbitrators: https://www.finra.org/arbitration-mediation/diversity

My article on the position of consumer groups on mandatory arbitration: https://www.huffpost.com/entry/finra-a-wily-fox-guarding_b_403552

The behavior gap: https://www.thebalancemoney.com/what-is-the-behavior-gap-2388311 and https://www.morningstar.com/funds/are-you-leaving-money-table-your-funds-returns.

Chapter 12: Letting Go

The chapter quote can be found at: https://www.goodreads.com/quotes/7588248-we-cannot-choose-our-external-circumstances-but-we-can-always.

Stoicism: https://iep.utm.edu/stoicism/

View of stoicism on dealing with what we can control: https://medium.com/stoicism-philosophy-as-a-way-of-life/the-importance-of-understanding-dichotomy-of-control-1f7133210c0d#:~:text=The%20Stoics%20believed%20that%20things,ourselves%20within%20a%20given%20situation

Stoic principle of accepting fate: https://medium.com/stoicism-philosophy-as-a-way-of-life/the-importance-of-understanding-dichotomy-of-control-1f7133210c0d#:~:text=The%20Stoics%20believed%20that%20things,ourselves%20within%20a%20given%20situation

Four stoic virtues: https://dailystoic.com/4-stoic-virtues/

Emotional intelligence and stoicism: https://medium.com/stoicism-philosophy-as-a-way-of-life/emotional-intelligence-and-stoicism-9175b91427ec#:~:text=Whether%20we're%20raging%2C%20hurt,nutshell%2C%20it%20teaches%20Emotional%20Intelligence

Quote from Lucius Annaeus Seneca: https://dailystoic.com/time-management/#:~:text=The%20amount%20of%20time%20we,it's%20our%20most%20valuable%20resource

Quote from Viktor Frankl: https://dailystoic.com/amor-fati/

Chapter 13: Perspective Power

The chapter quote can be found at: https://epgwealth.com.au/what-is-the-power-of-perspective-when-investing/#:~:text=Although%20it%20may%20be%20tempting,disciplined%20to%20your%20investment%20strategy.

Quote from Warren Buffett: https://www.trading212.com/learn/investing-101/active-vs-passive-investing

Survey of members of the Financial Planning Association: https://www.financialplanningassociation.org/sites/default/files/2021-03/AUG09%20The%20Changing%20Role%20of%20the%20Financial%20Planner%20Part%201%20From%20Financial%20Analytics%20to%20Coaching%20and%20Life%20Planning.pdf

Study on emotions: https://www.ncbi.nlm.nih.gov/pmc/articles/PMC8228195/#:~:text=Emotions%20arise%20from%20activations%20of,nucleus%2C%20and%20ventral%20tegmental%20area.

Amygdala hijack: https://www.ncbi.nlm.nih.gov/pmc/articles/PMC8228195/#:~:text=Emotions%20arise%20from%20activations%20of,nucleus%2C%20and%20ventral%20tegmental%20area.

Power of naming emotions: https://mindfulness.com/mindful-living/name-it-to-tame-it

Information about bull and bear markets: https://www.hartfordfunds.com/practice-management/client-conversations/managing-volatility/bear-markets.html#:~:text=A%20bear%20market%20doesn't,15%20recessions%20during%20that%20time.&text=Bear%20markets%20often%20go%20hand,mean%20a%20recession%20is%20looming.

Historical returns of the S&P 500 index: https://awealthofcommonsense.com/2022/12/how-often-is-the-market-down-in-consecutive-years/#:~:text=Since%201928%2C%20the%20S%26P%20500,time%20following%20a%20down%20year.

Chapter 14: Don't Look

The chapter quote can be found at: https://www.cnbc.com/select/how-often-should-you-check-your-investment-portfolio/.

Quotes attributed to Marcus Aurelius: https://donaldrobertson.name/2020/07/31/the-stoics-on-how-to-stop-doing-things/

The endowment effect: https://thedecisionlab.com/biases/endowment-effect?&adw=true&utm_campaign=21+Biases+-+Endowment+Effect&utm_medium=ppc&utm_source=adwords&utm_term=endowment%20effect&hsa_mt=b&hsa_net=adwords&hsa_ad=500704987890&hsa_src=g&hsa_cam=12413028140&hsa_kw=endowment%20effect&hsa_grp=121913746767&hsa_tgt=kwd-295792238609&hsa_ver=3&hsa_acc=8441935193&gad=1&gclid=CjwKCAjw2K6lBhBXEiwA5RjtCQqi-Sy3940_t7fm2cQ-AB5JXz7yx6xEzyfbhSsgVnumPVvSSll7lhoC-QsQAvD_BwE

Information bias: https://www.miraeassetmf.co.in/knowledge-center/information-bias#:~:text=Information%20bias%20is%20the%20tendency,did%20not%20have%20sufficient%20information

Harmful effects of too much cortisol: https://www.miraeassetmf.co.in/knowledge-center/information-bias#:~:text=Information%20bias%20is%20the%20tendency,did%20not%20have%20sufficient%20information

Chapter 15: Masterly Inactivity

The chapter quote can be found at: https://leomax89.medium.com/kindle-highlights-from-berkshire-hathaway-letters-to-shareholders-1965-2018-by-warren-buffet-8c1b86cbc00.

The focus of stoics on thoughts, beliefs, and actions: https://www.linkedin.com/pulse/from-fear-fearless-stoic-philosophy-managing-anxiety-goodman-ph-d-/

Bogle quote: https://www.forbes.com/sites/chrisbarth/2011/08/09/bogle-to-investors-dont-do-something-stand-there/?sh=79f734862b47

Peril of market timing: https://www.hartfordfunds.com/practice-management/client-conversations/managing-volatility/timing-the-market-is-impossible.html

2022 loss in value of VT: https://finance.yahoo.com/quote/VT/history/

2022 loss in value of SHY: https://finance.yahoo.com/quote/SHY/performance/

Recency bias: https://www.scribbr.com/research-bias/recency-bias/#:~:text=Recency%20bias%20is%20the%20tendency,how%20the%20future%20will%20unfold.

Herding behavior: https://www.ncbi.nlm.nih.gov/pmc/articles/PMC2827453/#:~:text=Herding%20can%20be%20defined%20as,of%20their%20own%2C%20private%20information.

Study on the impact of stress on London traders: https://www.reuters.com/article/uk-science-stress-markets/trader-stress-hormones-may-exacerbate-financial-market-crises-idUKLNEA1H00G20140218/

Confirmation bias: https://www.wallstreetmojo.com/confirmation-bias-examples/

Chapter 16: Don't Be Intimidated

The chapter quote can be found at: https://thefinancebuff.com/tax-efficient-asset-placement-difference.html.

Views of Stoics concerning simplicity: https://dailystoic.com/4-stoic-virtues/#:~:text=The%20Stoics%20shun%20complexity%20and,temperance%2C%20wisdom%2C%20and%20justice.

Discussion about rebalancing: https://www.investopedia.com/investing/rebalance-your-portfolio-stay-on-track/#:~:text=Why%20is%20rebalancing%20your%20portfolio,risk%20profile%20of%20your%20portfolio.

Quote from John Bogle: https://www.morningstar.com/articles/615379/bogle-be-sensible-about-rebalancing

Discussion about tax loss harvesting: https://www.fidelity.com/viewpoints/personal-finance/tax-loss-harvesting#:~:text=Tax%20loss%20harvesting%20allows%20you,invested%20and%20working%20for%20you.

"Wash sale" rule: https://www.fidelity.com/learning-center/personal-finance/wash-sales-rules-tax.

Discussion of $3000 offset from taxable income: https://www.schwab.com/learn/story/how-to-cut-your-tax-bill-with-tax-loss-harvesting

Discussion of asset location: https://www.whitecoatinvestor.com/asset-location/

Chapter 17: Ignore Naked Pundits

The chapter quote can be found at: https://papers.ssrn.com/sol3/papers.cfm?abstract_id=4390165.

Quote attributed to Seneca: https://www.stoicsimple.com/stoic-quotes-on-uncertainty-the-best-stoicism-sayings-phrases/

Study about the accuracy of stock market forecasts: https://papers.ssrn.com/sol3/papers.cfm?abstract_id=4390165

2008 median forecast from Wall Street "experts": https://www.nytimes.com/2019/12/23/business/retirement/index-fund-investing.html

Halo Effect: https://www.valuewalk.com/halo-effect-bias/

Tendency to ascribe positive traits to attractive people: https://link.springer.com/article/10.1007/s12144-022-03575-0#:~:text=Research%20has%20found%20that%20attractiveness,most%20research%20using%20western%20samples.

Availability heuristic: https://www.researchgate.net/publication/228419434_The_Availability_Heuristic_and_Investors'_Reaction_to_Company-Specific_Events

Impact of the availability heuristic on investing decisions: https://www.investopaper.com/news/availability-heuristic/

Chapter 18: Don't Look For Patterns

The chapter quote can be found at: https://www.linkedin.com/pulse/life-mars-money-tricks-our-brains-play-mitch-tuchman/.

Views of Stoics on finding false patterns: https://dailystoic.com/self-sufficiency-the-ultimate-stoic-virtue/

Unpredictability of stock price movements: https://www.aaii.com/journal/article/stock-price-movements-are-unpredictable

Study on the evolutionary origins of pattern-seeking: https://www.ncbi.nlm.nih.gov/pmc/articles/PMC4141622/

Study showing our subconscious effort to find patterns: https://www.ncbi.nlm.nih.gov/pmc/articles/PMC3749823/

How we are wired to find patterns: https://www.psychologytoday.com/us/blog/singular-perspective/202105/why-the-human-brain-is-so-good-detecting-patterns

Discussion of Apophenia: https://psychcentral.com/lib/patterns-the-need-for-order#examples

Impact on your brain of simply labeling something: https://www.wildpeace.org/name-it-to-tame-it-reframe#:~:text=Research%20has%20found%20that%20labeling,it%22%20to%20explain%20this%20phenomenon

Chapter 19: Real Love

The chapter quote can be found at: https://www.fidelity.com/viewpoints/financial-basics/financial-stability-and-love.

Discussion of the high rates of poverty of widows: https://www.ssa.gov/policy/docs/ssb/v65n3/v65n3p3l.html#:~:text=Poverty%20rates%20of%20widows%20decline,once%20they%20reach%20their%2080s

Chapter 20: The Hype and the Reality

The chapter quote can be found at: https://www.tataaia.com/blogs/life-insurance/what-are-the-advantages-and-disadvantages-of-financial-planning.html.

SMART goals: https://www.atlassian.com/blog/productivity/how-to-write-smart-goals

Chapter 21: Monte Carlo Analysis Can Be Misused

The chapter quote can be found at: https://www.linkedin.com/posts/michaelkitces_why-i-advocate-the-use-of-monte-carlo-analysis-activity-7024814064639836160-AKJP/.

Origin of the Monte Carlo simulation name: https://www.ibm.com/topics/monte-carlo-simulation#:~:text=The%20Monte%20Carlo%20Method%20was,to%20a%20game%20of%20roulette

Monte Carlo simulation: https://corporatefinanceinstitute.com/resources/financial-modeling/monte-carlo-simulation/

Study about the performance of different Monte Carlo models: https://www.kitces.com/blog/monte-carlo-models-simulation-forecast-error-brier-score-retirement-planning/

Benefits of using a Monte Carlo simulation in financial modeling: https://finmodelslab.com/blogs/blog/monte-carlo-simulation-financial-modelling

Monte Carlo simulation tool provided by Portfolio Visualizer: https://www.portfoliovisualizer.com/monte-carlo-simulation

Chapter 22: Entrepreneurial Courage

The chapter quote can be found at: https://www.goodreads.com/quotes/451403-whenever-you-see-a-successful-business-someone-once-made-a.

Study on entrepreneurship and millennials: https://startupnation.com/start-your-business/state-entrepreneurship-millennials/

Chapter 23: How Much is Enough

The chapter quote can be found at: https://www.bankrate.com/retirement/how-much-to-save-for-retirement/#:~:text=save%20small%20amounts.-,Retirement's%204%20percent%20rule,called%20the%204%20percent%20rule.

Story of Olive Swindells: https://www.latimes.com/archives/la-xpm-1995-12-28-mn-18717-story.html

Story of Ronald Read: https://finance.yahoo.com/news/janitor-vermont-amassed-8m-fortune-140000770.html#:~:text=Read%2C%20a%20retired%20gas%20station,much%20of%20Read's%20local%20community

Fidelity's guidelines for how much you should save for retirement: https://www.fidelity.com/viewpoints/retirement/how-much-do-I-need-to-retire

Fidelity's guidelines for how much you will spend in retirement: https://www.fidelity.com/viewpoints/retirement/spending-in-retirement#:~:text=Expect%20to%20spend%2055%25%E2%80%9380,current%20income%20annually%20in%20retirement

Life expectancy calculator of the Social Security Administration: https://www.ssa.gov/oact/population/longevity.html

The New England Centenarian calculator: https://www.bumc.bu.edu/centenarian/

Inflation rates in the U.S from 1960-2022: https://www.worlddata.info/america/usa/inflation-rates.php#:~:text=During%20the%20observation%20period%20from,year%20inflation%20rate%20was%204.0%25

Inflation rates over the past decade: https://www.forbes.com/sites/qai/2023/01/02/is-inflation-high-compared-to-years-past-breaking-down-inflation-rates-by-year/?sh=1817f2d6d7a2

Healthcare and education as long-term drivers of inflation: https://thehill.com/opinion/finance/591995-health-care-and-higher-education-key-drivers-of-long-term-inflation/

Chapter 24: The Role of Gratitude

The chapter quote can be found at: https://www.wealth-mode.com/blog/how-gratitude-helps-you-retire-early.

Quote from Marcus Aurelius: https://dailystoic.com/gratitude/

Study on the relationship between gratitude and subjective well-being: https://www.wealth-mode.com/blog/how-gratitude-helps-you-retire-early

Quote from Robert A. Emmons: https://www.nytimes.com/2023/06/08/well/mind/gratitude-health-benefits.html

Health benefits of gratitude: https://news.umich.edu/be-grateful-it-may-improve-your-health/

Discussion of how gratitude can help our finances: https://www.ig.ca/en/insights/how-gratitude-can-help-your-finances

Hedonic Treadmill theory: https://positivepsychology.com/hedonic-treadmill/

Adaptation-Level theory: https://link.springer.com/referenceworkentry/10.1007/978-94-007-0753-5_25

Dopamine explanation: https://www.webmd.com/mental-health/what-is-dopamine

Role of dopamine in reward: https://www.sciencedirect.com/science/article/abs/pii/S0165017398000198

Social comparison theory: https://positivepsychology.com/social-comparison/#:~:text=Instead%20of%20the%20desired%20effect,subsequently%20develop%20low%20self%2Desteem

Harmful impact of social comparison: https://psycnet.apa.org/record/1993-16069-001

Chapter 25: A Trap for the Unwary

The chapter quote can be found at https://retirementresearcher.com/navigating-one-greatest-risks-retirement-income-planning/.

Sequence of returns risk, including the example provided: https://www.schwab.com/learn/story/timing-matters-understanding-sequence-returns-risk

Historical stock market returns: https://www.officialdata.org/us/stocks/s-p-500/1926#:~:text=Stock%20market%20returns%20since%201926&text=This%20is%20a%20return%20on,%2C%20or%206.96%25%20per%20year.

Yearly returns of the S&P 500 index: https://www.slickcharts.com/sp500/returns

Chapter 26: Smoothing Over Savings

The chapter quote can be found at: https://www.bls.gov/careeroutlook/2013/fall/art02.pdf.

Savings goals recommended by Fidelity: https://www.fidelity.com/viewpoints/retirement/how-much-do-i-need-to-retire

Grace Groner's story: https://www.gronerfoundation.com/grace-s-story

The fable of the chessboard and the grain of rice: https://tanggram.medium.com/the-magic-of-compound-interest-7f4d6ca4583b#:~:text=%E2%80%9COh%20emperor%2C%20my%20wishes%20are,grains%20as%20the%20square%20before.%E2%80%9D

Life Cycle Hypothesis: https://www.richmondfed.org/publications/research/econ_focus/2016/q3-4/jargon_alert

Contrary view about consumption smoothing: https://www.whitecoatinvestor.com/consumption-smoothing-is-stupid/

Chapter 27: Modern Budgeting

The chapter quote can be found at: https://finlit.yale.edu/planning/budgeting-and-goal-setting.

You Need A Budget website: https://www.ynab.com/

Empower website: https://www.empower.com/empower-personal-wealth-transition?utm_medium=cpc&utm_source=google&utm_campaign=pcc_us_ggl_sem_branded_general_des_exact_all_all_all&utm_content=tools&utm_device=c&utm_term=personal%20capital%20budgeting&gad_source=1&gclid=CjwKCAi

PocketGuard website: https://pocketguard.com/

50-30-20 Rule: https://www.unfcu.org/guides/the-50-30-20-rule/#:~:text=The%2050%2D30%2D20%20rule%20recommends%20putting%2050%25%20of,closer%20look%20at%20each%20category

Health Savings Accounts: https://www.healthcare.gov/glossary/health-savings-account-hsa/

Flexible Spending Accounts: https://www.healthcare.gov/have-job-based-coverage/flexible-spending-accounts/

The debt snowball and avalanche methods for reducing debt: https://www.advantageccs.org/blog/which-debt-to-pay-off-first-debt-snowball-method-vs-debt-avalanche-method/?refppc=grant&kw=&creative=656463683405&gad_source=1&gclid=CjwKCAiA3aeqBhBzEiwAxFiOBs4MGvKnNeapdmho-HU98yJkcSwi7dMrB8PrXBzM7ymCdXWixiA0r4BoChiEQAvD_BwE

Chapter 28: Slay Student Loans

The chapter quote can be found at: https://dfpi.ca.gov/2023/02/13/student-loan-debt-a-disproportionate-burden-on-black-and-latino-borrowers/#:~:text=Millions%20of%20Americans%20are%20affected,highest%20consumer%20market%20after%20mortgages.

Average student loan debt: https://educationdata.org/average-student-loan-debt#:~:text=The%20average%20federal%20student%20loan,them%20have%20federal%20loan%20debt

Student loan interest rates: https://www.bankrate.com/loans/student-loans/current-interest-rates/

Federal Student Aid website: https://studentaid.gov/

SAVE repayment plan: https://studentaid.gov/announcements-events/save-plan

The Consolidated Appropriations Act of 2023 and how it impacts student loans: https://www.sequoia.com/2023/01/student-loan-legislation-what-employers-need-to-know/

SECURE 2.0 Act of 2022: https://www.bloomberglaw.com/external/document/XAUSB4C8000000/retirement-benefits-professional-perspective-secure-2-0-matching

Chapter 29: Tax Tricks

The chapter quote can be found at: https://www.nerdwallet.com/article/taxes/tax-planning.

Length of the U.S. tax code: https://www.vox.com/policy-and-politics/2017/3/29/15109214/tax-code-page-count-complexity-simplification-reform-ways-means

Basics of tax planning: https://www.nerdwallet.com/article/taxes/tax-planning

Importance of tax planning: https://www.bctax.com/blog/the-importance-of-tax-planning/#:~:text=With%20proper%20tax%20planning%2C%20you,you%20create%20your%20financial%20plan

Year-end tax planning strategies: https://www.abipcpa.com/year-end-tax-planning-strategies-for-individuals/#:~:text=General%20tax%20planning%20strategies%20for,charitable%20gifts%2C%20and%20retirement%20planning

Donor advised funds: https://www.fidelitycharitable.org/guidance/philanthropy/what-is-a-donor-advised-fund.html?immid=PCD&account=GOOGLE&campaign=Donor+Advised+Primer&adgroup=Donor+Advised&gad_source=1&gclid=CjwKCAiA8NKtBhBtEiwAq5aX2HxPpXcBzBk-4qBV3yJwqeS90aL3Ka-VTnAiXhcAul3z-H2pUw_7ohoCaZsQAvD_BwE&gclsrc=aw.ds

Requirements for becoming a CPA: https://www.accounting.com/careers/cpa/how-to-become/

CPAverify website: https://cpaverify.org/

American Institute of CPAs website: https://www.aicpa-cima.com/home

Personal Financial Specialist credential: https://us.aicpa.org/membership/join/pathway-pfs-credential.html

Chapter 30: Shortfalls

The chapter quote can be found at: https://money.usnews.com/investing/investing-101/articles/2018-08-20/6-ways-to-fix-a-retirement-savings-shortfall.

Cost of tiny homes: https://www.rocketmortgage.com/learn/how-much-does-a-tiny-house-cost#:~:text=The%20average%20cost%20of%20a,caught%20up%20in%20the%20savings

Discussion of the cheapest places to retire abroad: https://money.usnews.com/money/retirement/baby-boomers/slideshows/the-cheapest-places-to-retire-abroad-on-1-000-per-month

Chapter 31: Insurable Risks

The chapter quote can be found at: https://www.cfainstitute.org/en/membership/professional-development/refresher-readings/risk-management-individuals.

Discussion of how much life insurance you need: https://www.investopedia.com/articles/pf/06/insureneeds.asp#:~:text=Most%20insurance%20companies%20say%20a,child%20above%20the%2010x%20amount

Long-term care statistics: https://www.aplaceformom.com/senior-living-data/articles/long-term-care-statistics

Discussion of insurance company ratings: https://trustlayer.io/resources/why-does-your-insurance-companys-rating-matter

Chapter 32: A Mind-blowing Life Insurance Secret

The chapter quote can be found at: https://www.dfs.ny.gov/apps_and_licensing/insurance_companies/faqs/regulation_194.

List of fee-only insurance consultants: https://www.glenndaily.com/links.htm

Discussion of life insurance commissions: https://theinsuranceproblog.com/life-insurance-commission-a-great-evil-according-to-the-internet/

Insurance policy illustrations were provided by Chuck Hinners.

Chapter 33: Uninsurable Risks

The chapter quote can be found at: https://www.investopedia.com/terms/u/uninsurable-risk.asp#:~:text=Key%20Takeaways-,Uninsurable%20risk%20is%20a%20condition%20that%20poses%20an%20unknowable%20or,as%20coverage%20for%20criminal%20penalties.

Potential impact of artificial intelligence on jobs: https://www.bbc.com/news/technology-65102150

Annuities: https://institutional.vanguard.com/insights-and-research/report/annuities-and-tdfs-what-is-the-right-approach.html

Fixed annuities at: https://www.forbes.com/advisor/retirement/fixed-vs-index-annuity/

Variable annuities: https://www.investor.gov/introduction-investing/investing-basics/investment-products/insurance-products/variable-annuities

Indexed annuities: https://www.fidelity.com/viewpoints/retirement/considering-indexed-annuities

FINRA quote: https://www.finra.org/investors/insights/complicated-risks-and-rewards-indexed-annuities

Annuity offerings of Massachusetts Mutual Life Insurance Company: https://www.finra.org/investors/insights/complicated-risks-and-rewards-indexed-annuities

Annuity offerings of USAA Life Insurance Company: https://www.usaa.com/inet/wc/insurance_annuities_main?SearchRanking=1&SearchLinkPhrase=annuities

Annuity offerings New York Life Insurance Company: https://www.newyorklife.com/products/investments/annuities

Annuity offerings of TIAA-CREF Life Insurance Company: https://www.tiaa.org/public/retire/financial-products/annuities/annuitization

Chapter 34: Buy or Rent?

The chapter quote can be found at: https://www.nar.realtor/newsroom/middle-income-homeowners-gained-more-than-120000-in-wealth-over-the-past-decade-from-home-appreciation.

Amount the real estate industry spends on lobbying: https://www.opensecrets.org/industries/lobbying.php?cycle=All&ind=f10

Price-to-rent ratio and its impact on the "buy or rent" decision: https://smartasset.com/data-studies/price-to-rent-ratio-in-the-50-largest-us-cities-2022

Views of experts on renting if you will be moving in 5 years or less: https://www.cnbc.com/2015/08/04/what-to-know-about-renting-versus-buying-a-home.html

Survey of Consumer Finances by the Federal Reserve: https://papers.ssrn.com/sol3/papers.cfm?abstract_id=3716239

Harvard University study on the impact of home ownership on wealth accumulation among lower-income families and minorities: https://www.researchgate.net/publication/290015954_Is_homeownership_still_an_effective_means_of_building_wealth_for_low-income_and_minority_households

Negative view of some wealth advisors toward home ownership: https://www.cnbc.com/2019/04/18/wealth-manager-buying-a-home-is-usually-a-terrible-investment.html

Comparison of stock market returns to appreciation in home ownership: https://www.investopedia.com/ask/answers/052015/which-has-performed-better-historically-stock-market-or-real-estate.asp

Index used to make interest rate adjustments to adjustable rate mortgages: https://journalistsresource.org/economics/adjustable-rate-mortgages-explainer/

Dominance of fixed-rate mortgages: https://www.nber.org/papers/w24446

Preference for a 30-year term for fixed-rate mortgages: https://www.debt.org/real-estate/mortgages/30-year-fixed/#:~:text=With%20all%20this%20boosting%20it,backed%20mortgage%2Dguarantor%20Freddie%20Mac

Pros and cons of adjustable and fixed-rate mortgages: https://www.bankrate.com/mortgages/arm-vs-fixed-rate/

Typical adjustment and lifetime caps of adjustable rate mortgages: https://mortgageequitypartners.com/mortgage-products/adjustable-rate-mortgage-arm/#:~:text=Most%20ARMs%20have%20caps%20of,the%20life%20of%20the%20loan

Complexity of choosing the right type of mortgage: https://www.nber.org/papers/w9759

Research indicating that adjustable rate mortgages tend on average to have lower interest rates than fixed-rate mortgages: https://www.businessinsider.com/should-i-get-adjustable-rate-mortgage-yale-economic-research-2022-11

Views of the Urban Institute about the risks posed by adjustable rate mortgages: https://www.urban.org/urban-wire/should-borrowers-be-afraid-adjustable-rate-mortgages

Chapter 35: To Prepay or Not to Prepay?

The chapter quote can be found at: https://knowledge.wharton.upenn.edu/article/should-i-pay-off-my-mortgage-early-in-this-economy/.

Liquidity: https://www.thebalancemoney.com/liquidity-definition-ratios-how-its-managed-3305939

Pros and cons of paying off your mortgage before retirement: https://www.forbes.com/sites/kristinmckenna/2022/09/26/should-you-pay-off-your-mortgage-before-retirement/?sh=4e7e000872ef and https://www.schwab.com/learn/story/should-you-pay-off-mortgage-before-you-retire and: https://www.kiplinger.com/retirement/604813/im-retired-should-i-pay-off-my-mortgage

Quote from Professor Michael R. Roberts: https://knowledge.wharton.upenn.edu/article/should-i-pay-off-my-mortgage-early-in-this-economy/

Quote from Kiplinger: https://www.kiplinger.com/retirement/604813/im-retired-should-i-pay-off-my-mortgage

Chapter 36: Will Power

The chapter quote can be found at: https://www.heritagelawwi.com/what-are-the-potential-consequences-of-not-having-an-estate-plan#:~:text=Without%20a%20comprehensive%20estate%20plan,would%20not%20have%20chosen%20yourself.

Percentage of Americans who don't have a will: https://www.caring.com/caregivers/estate-planning/wills-survey/

Quote from Yair Dor-Ziderman: https://www.theguardian.com/science/2019/oct/19/doubting-death-how-our-brains-shield-us-from-mortal-truth

Study showing how the mind has an automatic tendency to avoid awareness of its mortality: https://www.sciencedirect.com/science/article/abs/pii/S1053811919306688

Percentage of women who become widows: https://www.bedelfinancial.com/75-of-women-become-widows

Average age of widows: https://www.9and10news.com/2019/09/30/healthy-living-modern-widow/#:~:text=When%20you%20think%20of%20someone,women%20become%20widowed%20every%20day.

Death rates of millennials: https://www.statista.com/statistics/241572/death-rate-by-age-and-sex-in-the-us/#:~:text=In%20the%20United%20States%20in,of%20the%20population%20for%20women

American College of Trust and Estate Counsel website: https://www.actec.org/

Chapter 37: Don't be a Stranger

The chapter quote can be found at: https://www.gobankingrates.com/money/financial-planning/how-often-you-should-review-your-financial-plan-advisor-advice/.

Financial plan updates: https://www.gobankingrates.com/money/financial-planning/how-often-you-should-review-your-financial-plan-advisor-advice/

What to include in an annual review of financial plans: https://www.investopedia.com/articles/financial-advisors/021016/top-tips-annual-client-financial-reviews.asp#:~:text=An%20annual%20review%20should%20go,planning%2C%20and%20life%20insurance%20policies.

Quote from Joseph Ferrari: https://www.washingtonpost.com/lifestyle/wellness/procrastinate-why-stop-advice/2021/07/09/13b7dc2c-e00e-11eb-9f54-7eee10b-5fcd2_story.html

Percentage of those who procrastinate to some degree: https://www.mindtools.com/a5plzk8/how-to-stop-procrastinating

Causes of procrastination: https://psychcentral.com/lib/learn-about-procrastination#Procrastination-Has-Many-Causes

Adverse health consequences of procrastination: https://www.sciencedirect.com/science/article/abs/pii/S0191886906004454

Tips for how to stop procrastinating: https://www.mindtools.com/a5plzk8/how-to-stop-procrastinating

Utility of "cocaine" and "kale" phones: https://www.dailymail.co.uk/sciencetech/article-12324329/Why-experts-say-key-healthy-relationship-phone-cocaine-kale-cell-combination.html

List of apps to help overcome procrastination: https://www.developgoodhabits.com/procrastination-apps-mfl/

List of goal tracking apps: https://clickup.com/blog/goal-tracking-apps/

List of meditation and mindfulness apps: https://positivepsychology.com/mindfulness-apps/

Chapter 38: Brain Barriers

The chapter quote can be found at: https://slate.com/technology/2017/04/why-people-are-so-bad-at-thinking-about-the-future.html.

Temporal discounting: https://www.frontiersin.org/articles/10.3389/fpsyg.2017.01007/full

Quote from Hal Hershfield: https://www.frontiersin.org/articles/10.3389/fpsyg.2017.01007/full

Power of accountability: https://www.afcpe.org/news-and-publications/the-standard/2018-3/the-power-of-accountability/#:~:text=The%20researchers%20found%20that%20individuals,you%20will%20do%20it%3A%2040%25

Chapter 39: Decoding Fees

The chapter quote can be found at: https://larrybates.ca/.

Difference in the standard of care owed to clients by RIAs and broker-dealers: https://www.investopedia.com/articles/active-trading/100915/rias-and-independent-brokerdealers-comparison.asp#:~:text=RIAs%20have%20a%20fiduciary%20duty,to%20meet%20the%20suitability%20standard

Commission-based advice: https://rpc.cfainstitute.org/en/policy/positions/commission-based-advice#sort=%40pubbrowsedate%20descending

Fee-only advice: https://www.investopedia.com/articles/investing/102014/feeonly-financial-advisers-what-you-need-know.asp#:~:text=A%20fee%20only%20financial%20advisor,products%20they%20sell%20or%20trade

Hidden conflicts of interest of fee-only financial advisors: https://community.acplanners.org/browse/blogs/blogviewer?BlogKey=88c07a0e-bb37-40ef-8642-3172716b0884

Fee calculator created by Larry Bates: https://larrybates.ca/t-rex-score/

Flat-fee model: https://www.yahoo.com/now/much-flat-fee-financial-advisors-134720141.html

Hourly-rate model: https://www.investopedia.com/ask/answers/091815/what-fees-do-financial-advisors-charge.asp

Performance-based model: https://www.investopedia.com/terms/p/performance-fee.asp#:~:text=A%20performance%20fee%20is%20a,often%20both%20realized%20and%20unrealized

Financial advisor minimums: https://smartasset.com/financial-advisor/the-minimum-investment-for-a-financial-advisor

Chapter 40: Cutting Costs

The chapter quote can be found at: https://investor.vanguard.com/investor-resources-education#:~:text=In%20other%20words%2C%20you%20don,end%20up%20with%20about%20%24430%2C000.

Betterment website: https://www.betterment.com/?utm_campaign=PMax&utm_content=brand&utm_medium=sem&gad_source=1&gclid=CjwKCAiAzc2tBhA6EiwArv-i6ZgNfMA0vCY9HqvNknGmZI7sHiJmH8Ep68f7Wg0_NBnFml75Swu_ZhoC3ygQAvD_BwE&gclsrc=aw.ds

Wealthfront website: https://www.wealthfront.com/?&utm_source=google&utm_medium=brand-search&utm_campaign=brand_exact-wf_ps-b_aw_all_dr_brand_20210825&cparam_campaignid=2061931427&utm_term=wealthfront&utm_content=null&cparam_contentid=601533116062&cparam_adgroup=null&cparam_adgroupid=76855954235&cparam_device=a&cparam_matchtype=e&campaignid=2061931427&adgroupid=76855954235&adid=601533116062&gclid=Cj0KCQjwi7GnBhDXARIsAFLvH4nla0fjqtLoCVCQSUTfvnlMiDmB_7PAv0uaxWtR9d87lg5ljX0sXPYaAibyEALw_wcB

Vanguard Digital Advisor website: https://investor.vanguard.com/advice/robo-advisor?cmpgn=RIG:PS:XXX:DA:10212021:GS:DM:BD_DA_Digital_Exact:NOTARG:NONE:DigitalAdvisor:Ad&gclid=Cj0KCQjwi7GnBhDXARIsAFLvH4kd3IM5xJaKwhRKk3VO990FlLoA6Vv38dw9J6YHldD8IDDe-Zgayu0aAvl_EALw_wc-B&gclsrc=aw.ds

Schwab Intelligent Portfolios website: https://www.schwab.com/intelligent-portfolios?src=SEM&ef_id=CjOKCQjwi7GnBhDXARIsAFLvH4m5K3XK-5WxfexWiz3Z6O-DUNZN-ki3lyO7nUvasffV7TJrIXoFD-aUaArtoEALw_wcB:G:s&s_kwcid=AL!5158!3!563641296915!e!!g!!schwab%20intelligent%20portfolio!65767217O!333938I5276&keywordid=kwd-88755627140&gclid=CjOKCQjwi7GnBhDXARIsAFLvH4m5K3XK5WxfexWiz3Z6O-DUNZN-ki3lyO7nUvasffV7TJrIXoFD-aUaArtoEALw_wcB

Fidelity GO website: https://www.fidelity.com/managed-accounts/fidelity-go/investment-account-faqs?imm_pid=700000001446522&immid=100725_SEA&imm_eid=ep77337760028&utm_source=GOOGLE&utm_medium=paid_search&utm_account_id=700000001446522&utm_campaign=DPA&utm_content=58700008485835953&utm_term=fidelity-go&utm_campaign_id=100725&utm_id=71700000112725739&gad=1&gclid=CjOKCQjwi7GnBhDXARIsAFLvH4IDsqyt89Pf_HuTjd8rJhPdoMDTZvAxxOVDoNGVM7GqgBK8OjuJcl0aAocvEALw_wcB&gclsrc=aw.ds

Vanguard Personal Advisors website: https://investor.vanguard.com/advice/personal-hybrid-robo-advisor

Schwab Intelligent Portfolios Premium website: https://www.schwab.com/intelligent-portfolios-premium

Garrett Planning Network website: https://www.garrettplanningnetwork.com/

XY Planning Network website: https://www.xyplanningnetwork.com/

NAPFA website: https://www.napfa.org/

Chapter 41: Studies that Quantify Value

The chapter quote can be found at: https://www.kitces.com/blog/trust-research-advisor-planner-use-benefits-value-vanguard-alpha-morningstar-gamma/.

2023 Russell Investments study:

https://russellinvestments.com/Publications/US/Document/Value_of_an_Advisor_Study.pdf

2022 Russell Investments study:

https://russellinvestments.com/us/blog/value-of-an-advisor-2022

2022 Vanguard study: https://advisors.vanguard.com/insights/article/putting-a-value-on-your-value-quantifying-advisors-alpha

2013 Morningstar study:

https://corporate.morningstar.com/ib/documents/PublishedResearch/AlphaBetaandNowGamma.pdf

Article authored by Derek Tharp, Ph.D.: https://www.kitces.com/blog/trust-research-advisor-planner-use-benefits-value-vanguard-alpha-morningstar-gamma/

Chapter 42: AI is Your New BFF

The chapter quote can be found at: https://www.investmentexecutive.com/news/industry-news/ai-could-make-financial-planning-more-accessible-suggest-some-in-the-sector/.

Discussion of the ways artificial intelligence will revolutionize the financial planning industry: https://www.forbes.com/sites/forbestechcouncil/2021/09/30/top-five-ways-ai-is-revolutionizing-the-financial-planning-industry/?sh=142304lc3f6d

PocketGuard website: https://pocketguard.com/

Cleo website: https://web.meetcleo.com/

Credit Karma website: https://www.creditkarma.com/

Experian website: https://www.experian.com/

Credit Sesame website: https://www.creditsesame.com/

Intuit Turbo Tax website: https://turbotax.intuit.com/?srqs=null&cid=ppc_gg_b_stan_all_na_Brand-BrandTTCore-TurboTax-Exact_ty22-bu2-sb5_63844941 4034_58623458533_kwd-26897251&srid=CjOKCQjwusunBhCYARIsAFBsUP9EFZLHxCuQAwuKcu6lzN3ARTb9LfjePGANqJ6vvV5Gcacd-ZGzT3AaAiyOEALw_wcB&targetid=kwd-26897251&skw=turbotax&adid=63844941 4034&ven=gg&gad=1&gclid=CjOKCQjwusunBhCYARIsAFBsUP9EFZLHxCuQAwuKcu6lzN3ARTb9LfjePGANqJ6vvV5Gcacd-ZGzT3AaAiyOEALw_wcB&gclsrc=aw.ds

H&R Block website: https://www.hrblock.com/lp/tax-filing/?https://www.hrblock.com/lp/tax-filing/?otppartnerid=9171&campaignid=ps_mcm_9171_7004_fy24_lob-gct_104_p07_a08_71700000089576942_587000075889033553_h%24r+block&gclid=CjOKCQjwusunBhCYARIsAFBsUP_XAbY_k5Gsu9JQ-U8M5lulwSCZeRMuy3HCU7XOBhY-lK_MUVv6aegaAt9XEALw_wcB&gclsrc=aw.ds

Shoeboxed website: https://www.shoeboxed.com/

Insurify website: https://insurify.com/

Portfolio Visualizer website: https://www.portfoliovisualizer.com/

Stockal website: https://stockal.com/

Coin Tracker website: https://www.cointracker.io/?utm_source=Google&utm_campaign=CT_BRAND_US_Brand&utm_medium=BRAND_US_Brand&utm_content=exact&utm_term=cointracker&gclid=CjOKCQjwgNanBhDUARIsAAelcAt3ehO3Gl2jl4LwbP47_9lAyr-lDcEofacAE70EsRWjThfHKiHQygYaAo09EALw_wcB

Streaks website: https://streaksapp.com/#:~:text=Streaks%20is%20the%20to%2Ddo,floss%20your%20teeth

Empower website:

https://www.empower.com/personal-investors/financial-tools

WealthTrace website:

https://www.mywealthtrace.com/

Quicken website:

https://www.quicken.com/lp/ppc/brand-simplifi/?utm_medium=cpc&utm_source=google&utm_campaign=%5bMM%5d-GGL_Search_Brand_Exact_USA_Consolidation&adgroup=quicken_starter&utm_term=quicken%20starter&utm_targetid=kwd-298171431297&utm_matchtype=e&coupon_code=&gclid=CjwKCAiA8NKtBhBtEiwAq5aX2HZPlkfkDJ5pi072Nc_dhyLmPRsGzNNq2Tux-jklqH_wjRdMD6yqkRoCUIOQAvD_BwE

ChatGPT: https://chat.openai.com/

Conclusion: Trust Yourself

The chapter quote can be found at: https://dailystoic.com/trust-yourself/.

Resources

My favorite investing books:

Berkin, Andrew L. and Swedroe, Larry E. *Your Complete Guide to Factor-Based Investing.* Buckingham. 2016.

Bernstein, William J. *If You Can: How Millennials Can Get Rich Slowly.* Efficient Frontier Publications, 2014.

Bogle, John C. *The Little Book of Common Sense Investing.* Wiley, 2017.

Carlson, Ben. *A Wealth of Common Sense.* 1st ed. Bloomberg Press. 2015

Ellis, Charles. *Winning the Loser's Game.* 8th ed. McGraw Hill. 2021

Housel, Morgan. *The Psychology of Money.* Harriman House, 2021.

Larimore, Taylor. *The Bogleheads' Guide to the Three-Fund Portfolio.* 1st ed. Wiley. 2018.

Swedroe, Larry E. and Kizer, Jared. *The Only Guide to Alternative Investments You'll Ever Need.* Bloomberg Press. 2008.

Swedroe, Larry E. and Adams, Samuel C. *Your Essential Guide to Sustainable Investing.* Harriman House. 2022.

My favorite books that will help you understand how your mind influences your behavior:

Dweck, Carol S. *Mindset: The New Psychology of Success.* Reprint ed. Random House Publishing Group. 2007.

Kahneman, Daniel. *Thinking, Fast and Slow.* 1st ed. Farrar, Straus and Giroux. 2011.

Medina, John. *Brain Rules.* 1st ed. Pear Press. 2020.

Pigliucci, Massimo. *How to Be a Stoic.* Reprint ed. Basic Books. 2018.

Sacks, Oliver. *Gratitude.* Illustrated ed. Knopf. 2015.

Thaler, Richard H. *Misbehaving, The Making of Behavioral Economics.* Reprint ed. W.W. Norton & Company. 2016.

This book provides advice you won't find anywhere else on buying life insurance:

Hinners, Chuck. *Insider Trading in the Life Insurance Market: A Smart Buyer's Guide.* CreateSpace Independent Publishing Platform. 2015

AI Disclosure

I used artificial intelligence (mainly ChatGPT 4.0) for basic research.

In some instances, I used text generated by ChatGPT, but rarely without editing it.

I checked all facts generated by artificial intelligence and independently sourced them in the Endnotes.

All opinions are mine alone.

Index

Adaptation-Level Theory, 134
advisor/advisory
    fees, 36, 148-50, 163, 174, 194-97
    financial, 14-17, 148, 150-51, 200-205
    robo, 198-200
    services, 45
AI (artificial intelligence), 166, 204, 207
allocations, 16, 37-39, 44-46, 54, 100-102, 119, 131, 136-38, 151-52
Almeda, Max Leonard, 97
alternative investments
    cryptocurrency, 61
    hedge funds, 18, 36, 54, 197
    funds, 43, 45, 110, 163
    investments, 15, 18-19, 48-49, 167
    role of, 36
amygdala, 11, 19, 91-93
analysis/analyze
    financial, 43, 48, 80, 95, 98, 204-05, 148, 168-69
    Monte Carlo, 26, 119-22
    technical, 66-68
    trend, 108
annuity, 47, 167-69, 196
apophenia, 19, 109-10
applications (apps), 21, 26, 72, 144, 189, 194, 204-05
arbitration, 25, 27-28, 80-81, 91,
artificial intelligence. *See* AI, 166, 204-05, 221
assets
    allocation, 45-46, 100-103, 131, 136, 139, 168-69, 185
    depreciation, 58
    digital, 55-56
    distorting, 71
    location, 103-04, 119, 128, 202, 205
    ownership, 16, 54, 115-17, 184, 56, 157-58
    protection, 39, 149, 170-72
    safe-haven for, 65
    value, 21-23, 42, 48, 50-51, 58, 89-90, 98, 175-79, 197-99, 205-07
Baker, Brian, 129
bear market, 19-21, 92
behavior, 9, 19, 24-25, 32, 59-60, 80-81, 95-99, 108, 160, 190, 206
benchmark, 13, 20, 33, 35-37, 45-46, 49, 66
Bernstein, William J., 32-33
bias
    confidence, 16, 22, 25, 60, 69
    defined, 80-81, 95, 99, 106-07, 120, 159, 203

Binance, 62-63
Bitcoin. *See* cryptocurrency
Bankman-Fried, Sam, 62
Bogle, John, 33-34, 97, 101
bonds
    foreign, 37
    municipal, 104, 150
    portfolio, 16, 28, 32-39, 62, 174
    returns, 23, 131, 137-38, 178
    trading, 45-46, 54-55, 98-102
    treasury, 20-21, 34, 37
broker, 13, 25, 36, 43-45, 79, 90-93, 104, 158-59, 194-95
budget/budgeting, 46, 117-18, 124, 143-44, 151, 159, 185, 188-49, 204
Buffett, Warren, 32, 36, 61, 89, 97
bull market, 19, 20-21, 92
certificate of deposit, 37
Chidester, Justin, 132
China, 63
Choi, James, 68-69
climate change, 48, 50, 63, *See also,* global temperatures
Cohan, William D., 80
collectibles, 54-56, 58
commodities, 15-16, 18-19, 33, *See also* alternative investments
consequences, 15, 71-73, 95, 102, 166, 184, 198
costs, 198-200
Consolidated Appropriations Act of 2023, 146-147
contribution, 26-27, 43-47, 87, 100, 119, 142, 147-50, 177
Cryptocurrency
    Bitcoin, 61-63
    description of, 15, 18, 61
    mining, 21, 63
    types of, 56-57, 96, 205
    See also alternative investments
Custodio, Mariana, 56, 72
day trading, 33, 65-66
debt
    burden of, 114-17, 145-46, 152, 162
    consumer, 35, 64, 76-78, 141
    definition of, 20
    incurring, 130-31, 141-47, 169, 207
    issue of, 35, 90, 130, 177-79
    and net worth, 116-17, 156-57, 169
Democritus, 94
digital, 21, 55-57, 62, 199
discount(ing), 20, 161, 165, 190-91, 199-200
dividends, 82, 96, 104, 139

diversify, 16, 27, 34-37, 45, 69, 82-83, 167, 174
diversification
    investment, 21, 38, 50-51, 54-57, 62, 82-83
    portfolio, 16, 26-27, 34, 62, 69, 82
DIY (Do It Yourself)
    investing, 14-17, 39-41, 54, 79, 101-04, 106-110, 146, 164, 198, 202-07
    Monte Carlo, 121
    planning, 112-15, 117, 122-23, 131, 160, 184-85, 200
    taxes, 102-05, 204
Dopamine, 22, 60, 95, 134
Dor-Ziderman, Yair, 184
Drucker, Peter F., 122
EarthJustice, 62
economics, 65, 87, 117, 131-32, 141, 167, 177, 187-88
education, 87, 115, 130, 146-47, 150-51, 157, 166
Edwards, Benjamin P., 90
Egan, Dan, 94
Ellis, Charles D., 64
employer, employment, 43-47, 143, 146-47, 157, 167, 191
employee, 43-47, 143-44, 150, 156
Employee Benefit Research Institute, 76, 139
endowment, 22, 95
entrepreneur, 43, 46-47, 113-15, 122-25
environmental, social, and governance-based. *See.* ESG
Epictetus, 86
equity, 18, 26, 36, 41-42, 54, 57, 76, 83, 137, 162, 173
ESG, environmental, social, and governance-based investing, 22, 48-51
ESGV, 51
ETF, exchange traded fund
    investment, 27, 32-34, 37, 41-42, 48-51, 67, 103-04, 209
    managing, 18, 22-23, 25, 33-39, 44-46, 56, 81, 98
ethics, ethical, 48, 96, 150, 161, 196
evaluate/evaluation, 25, 49, 67, 95, 107, 120, 124, 135-36
exchange-traded fund. *See* ETF
factor-based investing, 22-23, 40-42
fees, 36, 45, 194-97
finance/financial
    advisor, 14-17, 32, 36, 45, 103, 141, 194-99, 200-203
    concepts, 18-19, 22, 48, 56-57, 96
    empowerment, 13-15, 73, 79, 151
    goals, 36-38, 40, 58-59, 63, 66-68, 98, 124-25, 128-29, 144, 156-57
    misinformation and myths, 69-70, 99, 105
    planning, 17, 24-25, 32, 35, 87, 114-21, 123, 136, 184-90, 206-07
    real estate, 172-74, 177-79
    situations, 76-78, 90-91, 110, 133, 143, 148-50, 152, 158, 161, 166-69
    sources, 23, 71-72, 95, 105-06, 139, 168-69, 203-05, 209
    systems, 80-82, 87, 130, 151-52

Financial Industry Regulatory Authority. *See* FINRA
Financial Planning Association, 90
FINRA, 25, 80-81, 168,
Fidelity Investments, 114, 129-30
forecasting, 87, 105-06, 116
FSA (Flexible Spending Account), 143
FTSE, 37, 46, 51
funds
    discretionary, 61, 117, 137, 144, 152-53, 157, 162, 202, 209
    ESG, 49-50
    ETF, 22, 27, 33-39, 37, 41-46, 48-51, 56, 67, 103-04, 98, 209
    hedge, 36, 54, 197
    HSA, 47
    index, 13-14, 18, 22-25, 33-34, 43, 45-46, 97, 174
    managed, 20, 22, 24-25, 50, 67-68, 77, 104, 120, 167, 168
    mutual, 17-18, 32-33, 44-45, 48-49, 69, 81-82, 104, 195
    retirement, 28, 63, 100, 102, 178
    traded, 16, 18
    yield, 117-18
Garrett Planning Network, 199
Gen Z, 48
gig economy, 143
Gillespie, Lane, 76
global temperatures. *See also* climate change, 48
goals
    apps for, 189
    financial, 36-38, 40, 51, 58-59, 63, 66-68, 98, 116, 124-25, 128-29, 144-45, 156-57
    long-term, 24-25, 28, 81, 87, 116-19, 123-25, 136, 147, 167-69, 187-89, 194
    personal, 13-17, 49, 61, 72, 79, 123, 134, 141-44, 150-51, 190-91, 199, 201, 205-07
Goldman Sachs, 41
gratitude/gratification, 60, 132-35
greenwashing, 24, 49
Groner, Grace, 139-40
Health Savings Account. *See* HSA
Hale, John, 49
Halo Effect, 106-07
He, Songrun, 106
Hedonic Treadmill, 134
hedge funds. *See also* alternative investments, 18, 36, 54, 197
Helson, Harry, 134
Hershfield, Hal, 191
heuristic, 107
Hinners, Chuck, 163
Ho, Nhung, 204
HSA (Health Savings Account), 24, 45, 47, 143, 149
index funds, 13-14, 18, 22-25, 33-34, 43, 45-46, 97, 174

Individual Retirement Account. *See* IRA
inflation, 38, 54, 57, 62, 65, 69, 82, 116, 119, 129-31, 173-75, 188
Insider Trading in the Life Insurance Market (Hinners), 163
insurance
    annuity, 47, 167-69, 196
    health, 156-57
    life, 118, 137, 157-58, 161-65, 169, 184
    term, 27, 162
    universal, 20, 28, 163-65
    whole life, 20, 28, 162-63
intellectual property, 57, 124
Intelligent Asset Allocator (Bernstein), 32
Insider Trading in the Life Insurance Market, (Hinners), 163
interest
    compound, 21, 139-40
    debt, 145-47, 152, 177-78
    mortgage, 149, 173-76
    rates, 20, 34, 38, 56, 64, 69, 87, 104-06, 116, 120, 163, 168, 188, 207
investment
    alternative, investments, 15, 18-19, 54-55, 58
    applications, 206-07
    diversification, 21, 38, 50-51, 54-57, 62, 82-83,
    ESG, 22, 48-51
    factor-based, 23-24, 40-42
    fractional, 55-56
    myths, 64-70, 99, 105
    responsible, 16, 19, 22, 24, 35-39, 48-51, 96, 115
    retirement, 26-28, 43-48, 63, 76-81, 103-05, 152, 190-91
    return on, 15-16, 22-28, 37, 65, 68, 82-83, 104, 129, 131, 134, 136, 179, 201
    security, 21-23, 28, 33, 37-38, 48-49, 55, 59-62, 102-03, 115, 175-77
    stock market, 23, 34-37, 54, 57, 66, 71-72, 92-93, 96-97, 106, 109, 179, 188
investor
    consequences, 71-72, 98, 106, 156
    DIY, 14-17, 21, 39-42, 54-55, 79, 101-04, 106-110, 146, 164, 198, 200-207
    myths, 64-70
    strategies, 22-27, 32-33, 36-38, 50, 58, 62, 80-83, 94-95, 108, 124, 137, 162-63
IRA
    Traditional, 27-28, 45-46, 104
    Retirement, 143, 149
    Roth, 28, 46, 149, 178, 103, 207
    SEP, 47
    Simple, 47
Kitces, Michael, 40, 119, 201
Lamas, Samantha, 13
Lambe, Brendan John, 71
Li, Jaien, 105

Life Cycle Hypothesis (LCH), 141
life
    expectancy, 116, 130
    insurance, 20, 27-28, 118, 137, 157-58, 161-65, 169, 184
liquidity, 20, 57-59, 82-83, 178, 180
loans
    applying for, 124, 175
    student, 77, 141, 145-47
lobbies/lobbying, 80-81, 172
longevity, 129, 167
loss
    aversion, 25, 95
    of investment, 23-24, 58, 60
    of liquidity, 180
    realized, 98, 137, 161, 178
    tax loss harvesting, 100, 102-04. 206
    yields, 65
Lynch, Peter, 26
Marcus Aurelius, 94, 96, 132
markets
    bear, 19, 21, 92
    bull, 19, 21, 92
    cap, 36-37, 40-41, 46, 51
McGonigal, Jane, 190
Merrill Lynch, 36-37, 46
millennials
    and debt, 76-78, 140-41
    as entrepreneurs, 122-23
    identification of, 14-16, 20-21, 54, 167
    investments by, 32-33, 48-51, 58, 103-04, 151
misinformation, 16, 69, 71-73, 81, 99, 100
money
    borrowing, 64-65
    decisions, 13-14, 18, 72, 82, 114-15, 172
    and emotion, 89-91
    investments, 14-15, 23, 34-37, 54, 57, 66, 195
    laundering, 56, 62-63
    lending, 35
    liquidity, 20, 57-59, 82-83, 178, 180
    manager, 13, 18, 36, 45
    map, 117-18
    saving, 43-46, 69, 120-21, 128-30, 133, 167, 176, 191
    tactics, 79, 86-87, 137, 152
    and taxes, 46, 148-49, 169
    volatility, 87

Monte Carlo Analysis, 26, 119-21, 202
Morningstar, 13, 38, 44, 49, 54, 81
mortgage, 77, 149, 173-80, 196
multifactor ETF, 41-42
mutual funds, 17-18, 32-33, 44-45, 48-49, 69, 81-82, 104, 195
Mukunda, Gautam, 79
network(ing), 167, 200
net worth, 15, 54, 56, 117, 163, 172, 174
New England Centenarian Study, 130-31
NTF, 54-56
Nonfungible Token. *See* NTF
Olin, John M., 106
Orman, Suze, 68
Patrick, Jordan, 187
patterns, 16, 19, 56, 66, 108-110, 141
performance
    investment, 13, 15-16, 20-28, 37-40, 56, 82-83, 104, 129, 131, 134-36, 168
    portfolio, 65, 68, 195-97, 205-06
    security, 23, 27, 94, 120, 179, 201
perspective, 89-93, 110, 133-34
Pfau, Wade, 136
phone
    cocaine, 21, 25, 189
    kale, 21, 25, 188-89
PocketGuard, 204
portfolio
    bond, 16, 28, 32-39, 62, 174
    diversified, 16, 26-27, 34, 62, 69, 82, 174
    factor-based, 101, 136-37
    performance, 54-58, 65, 68, 92, 97, 128-29, 178, 187, 195-99, 205-06
    simulation, 121
    stock, 27, 32, 36, 40-42, 49-50, 107, 119, 151
    value, 50, 94-96, 98-99, 100-103, 131, 136-38, 196
philosophy, 33, 86, 88, 94, 105
plans (401 (k), 403 (b), 457 (b)), 43-46, 89, 104, 115-17
platforms, 44, 55-58, 62, 198-99, 205
private equity. *See also* alternative investments
procrastination, 16, 188, 191
Ramsey, Dave, 69
ratios, 23, 37-38, 41-45, 47, 51, 174, 202
Read, Ronald, 128-29
real estate, 172
Rekenthaler, John, 54
research, 13, 23, 41, 44, 58, 65-67, 70, 123, 153, 176, 188, 201-03, 209

retirement
    accounts, 14, 26-28, 102-103, 117
    goals, 16, 69, 81, 116, 152, 190-91
    investing, 43-48
    plans
        401 (k), 43-46, 89, 104
        403 (b), 43
        457 (b), 43
    savings, 14, 27, 43-45, 76-77, 63, 115-17, 151-53
Retirement Researcher, 71-72
returns
    on investment, 15-16, 22-28, 37, 65, 68, 82-83, 104, 129, 131, 134, 136, 179, 201
    risk and, 35-38, 87, 100-102, 123-25
risk
    definition, 38-39
    insurable, 156-60
    vs. reward, 35-38, 87, 100-102, 123-25
    tolerance, 129, 137-38, 155
    types of, 20-21, 41, 45, 48-51, 56-60, 64, 66-69, 72, 80-82, 118-21,129
    uninsurable, 166-67
Roberts, Michael B., 177
Roth. *See* IRA
Royal, James, 128
royalties, 57
S&P 500, 18, 20, 49-51, 67, 82, 89, 92, 97, 136, 168, 174
savings
    health, 24, 45, 47, 143, 149
    plans, 87, 103, 119, 129-30 139-43, 147, 158, 162-63, 167, 191, 206
    retirement, 14, 27, 43-45, 69, 76-77, 63, 151-53
Schwab, Charles, 45, 63, 137, 199
SEC, 49, 62, 80
security/securities
    industry, 14-20, 27-28, 40, 49, 79-80, 99, 132, 172, 177
    investments, 21-23, 28, 33, 37-38, 48-49, 55, 59-62, 102-03, 115, 175-77
    performance, 23
Security and Exchange Commission. *See* SEC
sequence, 131, 136-38
Shrestha, Keshab, 71
Sit, Harry, 100
social media, 15, 124, 135, 189
socially responsible investing, *See.* ESG
Social Security, 77, 116, 130
speculate/speculation, 34, 62-63
spending, 57, 76, 90, 117, 130, 133, 141-44, 151-52, 178, 202-06
SPIVA Reports, 67
Stanford University, 50

stock market
    investing in, 14-15, 23, 34-37, 54, 57, 66
    movements in, 71-72, 82, 92-93, 96-97, 106, 109, 179, 188
    shares, 26-27, 40, 57, 139, 184
stoic, stoicism, 86-89, 93-94, 100, 105, 132
strategies
    investment, 50, 58, 62, 80-83, 94-95, 108, 124, 137, 162-63
    tax, 22-27, 32-33, 36-38
Swedroe, Larry, 40
Swindells, Olive, 128
taxes
    benefits, 57, 173
    fees, 18, 24-28, 33, 45-47, 101, 143, 146, 162-63
    income, 79, 150
    laws, 116-17, 149, 188
    paying, 17, 56, 124, 179, 187, 207
    planning, 187, 201-02, 205-07
    property, 152, 173
    tax loss harvesting, 100, 102-04
    tricks, 149-151
    withholding, 33, 46, 149
Tharp, Derek, 201, 203
The 9 Steps to Financial Freedom, (Orman), 68
Total Money Makeover, (Ramsey), 69
theories, 19, 134-35, 141
trading, 22, 33-34, 37, 41, 44, 57, 63-66, 72, 82, 163
treasury
    bills, 28, 34-35, 42, 66-67, 69, 178
    bonds, 20, 37
truth, 64-68
Tuchman, Mitch, 108
United States Government, 20, 28, 35, 62, 146-47
United States Treasury, 28, 34, 37, 46, 175
value
    cash, 20, 28, 137, 162-65, 196
    determine, 56, 88-89
    factors, 19, 23, 26, 49, 61-63, 76, 82, 97, 139, 173, 180, 194-97
    investing, 36, 148, 202-03
    portfolio, 94-95, 98-99, 101, 136-37
    quantifying, 201-203
    stocks, 41, 93, 102
VanDerhei, Jack, 139
Vanguard Group, 13, 33, 39, 45, 51, 97, 198-99, 202
vested 79, 172
volatility, 14-16, 23, 28, 37-38, 41-42, 46, 54-55, 63, 66, 87, 94-95, 98, 101, 119-120, 129, 151
Wall Street, 13, 36, 48, 106

Weaver, Jessica, 151
Wharton School of Economics, 177
Wisniewski, Thomas Piotr, 71
withdraw/withdrawal, 27-28, 46, 104, 121, 136-37, 149-50, 169
Witt, Scott, 163
workforce. *See* employee
Yahoo Finance, 23
Yale University, 68-69, 143
yield, 20, 23, 36, 66, 79, 117-18, 174-75
Yun, Lawrence, 172
Zhao, Changpeng, 63
Zhou, Guofu , 104

Made in the USA
Columbia, SC
21 May 2024